FREE Test Taking Tips DVD Offer

To help us better serve you, we have developed a Test Taking Tips DVD that we would like to give you for FREE. **This DVD covers world-class test taking tips that you can use to be even more successful when you are taking your test.**

All that we ask is that you email us your feedback about your study guide. Please let us know what you thought about it – whether that is good, bad or indifferent.

To get your **FREE Test Taking Tips DVD**, email freedvd@studyguideteam.com with "FREE DVD" in the subject line and the following information in the body of the email:

a. The title of your study guide.

b. Your product rating on a scale of 1-5, with 5 being the highest rating.

c. Your feedback about the study guide. What did you think of it?

d. Your full name and shipping address to send your free DVD.

If you have any questions or concerns, please don't hesitate to contact us at freedvd@studyguideteam.com.

Thanks again!

AP English Language and Composition 2019 & 2020

AP Language and Composition Test Prep 2019 & 2020 and Practice Test Questions for the Advanced Placement English Language & Composition Test [Includes Detailed Answer Explanations]

Test Prep Books

Table of Contents

Quick Overview

As you draw closer to taking your exam, effective preparation becomes more and more important. Thankfully, you have this study guide to help you get ready. Use this guide to help keep your studying on track and refer to it often.

This study guide contains several key sections that will help you be successful on your exam. The guide contains tips for what you should do the night before and the day of the test. Also included are test-taking tips. Knowing the right information is not always enough. Many well-prepared test takers struggle with exams. These tips will help equip you to accurately read, assess, and answer test questions.

A large part of the guide is devoted to showing you what content to expect on the exam and to helping you better understand that content. In this guide are practice test questions so that you can see how well you have grasped the content. Then, answer explanations are provided so that you can understand why you missed certain questions.

Don't try to cram the night before you take your exam. This is not a wise strategy for a few reasons. First, your retention of the information will be low. Your time would be better used by reviewing information you already know rather than trying to learn a lot of new information. Second, you will likely become stressed as you try to gain a large amount of knowledge in a short amount of time. Third, you will be depriving yourself of sleep. So be sure to go to bed at a reasonable time the night before. Being well-rested helps you focus and remain calm.

Be sure to eat a substantial breakfast the morning of the exam. If you are taking the exam in the afternoon, be sure to have a good lunch as well. Being hungry is distracting and can make it difficult to focus. You have hopefully spent lots of time preparing for the exam. Don't let an empty stomach get in the way of success!

When travelling to the testing center, leave earlier than needed. That way, you have a buffer in case you experience any delays. This will help you remain calm and will keep you from missing your appointment time at the testing center.

Be sure to pace yourself during the exam. Don't try to rush through the exam. There is no need to risk performing poorly on the exam just so you can leave the testing center early. Allow yourself to use all of the allotted time if needed.

Remain positive while taking the exam even if you feel like you are performing poorly. Thinking about the content you should have mastered will not help you perform better on the exam.

Once the exam is complete, take some time to relax. Even if you feel that you need to take the exam again, you will be well served by some down time before you begin studying again. It's often easier to convince yourself to study if you know that it will come with a reward!

Test-Taking Strategies

1. Predicting the Answer

When you feel confident in your preparation for a multiple-choice test, try predicting the answer before reading the answer choices. This is especially useful on questions that test objective factual knowledge. By predicting the answer before reading the available choices, you eliminate the possibility that you will be distracted or led astray by an incorrect answer choice. You will feel more confident in your selection if you read the question, predict the answer, and then find your prediction among the answer choices. After using this strategy, be sure to still read all of the answer choices carefully and completely. If you feel unprepared, you should not attempt to predict the answers. This would be a waste of time and an opportunity for your mind to wander in the wrong direction.

2. Reading the Whole Question

Too often, test takers scan a multiple-choice question, recognize a few familiar words, and immediately jump to the answer choices. Test authors are aware of this common impatience, and they will sometimes prey upon it. For instance, a test author might subtly turn the question into a negative, or he or she might redirect the focus of the question right at the end. The only way to avoid falling into these traps is to read the entirety of the question carefully before reading the answer choices.

3. Looking for Wrong Answers

Long and complicated multiple-choice questions can be intimidating. One way to simplify a difficult multiple-choice question is to eliminate all of the answer choices that are clearly wrong. In most sets of answers, there will be at least one selection that can be dismissed right away. If the test is administered on paper, the test taker could draw a line through it to indicate that it may be ignored; otherwise, the test taker will have to perform this operation mentally or on scratch paper. In either case, once the obviously incorrect answers have been eliminated, the remaining choices may be considered. Sometimes identifying the clearly wrong answers will give the test taker some information about the correct answer. For instance, if one of the remaining answer choices is a direct opposite of one of the eliminated answer choices, it may well be the correct answer. The opposite of obviously wrong is obviously right! Of course, this is not always the case. Some answers are obviously incorrect simply because they are irrelevant to the question being asked. Still, identifying and eliminating some incorrect answer choices is a good way to simplify a multiple-choice question.

4. Don't Overanalyze

Anxious test takers often overanalyze questions. When you are nervous, your brain will often run wild, causing you to make associations and discover clues that don't actually exist. If you feel that this may be a problem for you, do whatever you can to slow down during the test. Try taking a deep breath or counting to ten. As you read and consider the question, restrict yourself to the particular words used by the author. Avoid thought tangents about what the author *really* meant, or what he or she was *trying* to say. The only things that matter on a multiple-choice test are the words that are actually in the question. You must avoid reading too much into a multiple-choice question, or supposing that the writer meant something other than what he or she wrote.

5. No Need for Panic

It is wise to learn as many strategies as possible before taking a multiple-choice test, but it is likely that you will come across a few questions for which you simply don't know the answer. In this situation, avoid panicking. Because most multiple-choice tests include dozens of questions, the relative value of a single wrong answer is small. As much as possible, you should compartmentalize each question on a multiple-choice test. In other words, you should not allow your feelings about one question to affect your success on the others. When you find a question that you either don't understand or don't know how to answer, just take a deep breath and do your best. Read the entire question slowly and carefully. Try rephrasing the question a couple of different ways. Then, read all of the answer choices carefully. After eliminating obviously wrong answers, make a selection and move on to the next question.

6. Confusing Answer Choices

When working on a difficult multiple-choice question, there may be a tendency to focus on the answer choices that are the easiest to understand. Many people, whether consciously or not, gravitate to the answer choices that require the least concentration, knowledge, and memory. This is a mistake. When you come across an answer choice that is confusing, you should give it extra attention. A question might be confusing because you do not know the subject matter to which it refers. If this is the case, don't eliminate the answer before you have affirmatively settled on another. When you come across an answer choice of this type, set it aside as you look at the remaining choices. If you can confidently assert that one of the other choices is correct, you can leave the confusing answer aside. Otherwise, you will need to take a moment to try to better understand the confusing answer choice. Rephrasing is one way to tease out the sense of a confusing answer choice.

7. Your First Instinct

Many people struggle with multiple-choice tests because they overthink the questions. If you have studied sufficiently for the test, you should be prepared to trust your first instinct once you have carefully and completely read the question and all of the answer choices. There is a great deal of research suggesting that the mind can come to the correct conclusion very quickly once it has obtained all of the relevant information. At times, it may seem to you as if your intuition is working faster even than your reasoning mind. This may in fact be true. The knowledge you obtain while studying may be retrieved from your subconscious before you have a chance to work out the associations that support it. Verify your instinct by working out the reasons that it should be trusted.

8. Key Words

Many test takers struggle with multiple-choice questions because they have poor reading comprehension skills. Quickly reading and understanding a multiple-choice question requires a mixture of skill and experience. To help with this, try jotting down a few key words and phrases on a piece of scrap paper. Doing this concentrates the process of reading and forces the mind to weigh the relative importance of the question's parts. In selecting words and phrases to write down, the test taker thinks about the question more deeply and carefully. This is especially true for multiple-choice questions that are preceded by a long prompt.

9. Subtle Negatives

One of the oldest tricks in the multiple-choice test writer's book is to subtly reverse the meaning of a question with a word like *not* or *except*. If you are not paying attention to each word in the question, you can easily be led astray by this trick. For instance, a common question format is, "Which of the following is...?" Obviously, if the question instead is, "Which of the following is not...?," then the answer will be quite different. Even worse, the test makers are aware of the potential for this mistake and will include one answer choice that would be correct if the question were not negated or reversed. A test taker who misses the reversal will find what he or she believes to be a correct answer and will be so confident that he or she will fail to reread the question and discover the original error. The only way to avoid this is to practice a wide variety of multiple-choice questions and to pay close attention to each and every word.

10. Reading Every Answer Choice

It may seem obvious, but you should always read every one of the answer choices! Too many test takers fall into the habit of scanning the question and assuming that they understand the question because they recognize a few key words. From there, they pick the first answer choice that answers the question they believe they have read. Test takers who read all of the answer choices might discover that one of the latter answer choices is actually *more* correct. Moreover, reading all of the answer choices can remind you of facts related to the question that can help you arrive at the correct answer. Sometimes, a misstatement or incorrect detail in one of the latter answer choices will trigger your memory of the subject and will enable you to find the right answer. Failing to read all of the answer choices is like not reading all of the items on a restaurant menu: you might miss out on the perfect choice.

11. Spot the Hedges

One of the keys to success on multiple-choice tests is paying close attention to every word. This is never truer than with words like almost, most, some, and sometimes. These words are called "hedges" because they indicate that a statement is not totally true or not true in every place and time. An absolute statement will contain no hedges, but in many subjects, the answers are not always straightforward or absolute. There are always exceptions to the rules in these subjects. For this reason, you should favor those multiple-choice questions that contain hedging language. The presence of qualifying words indicates that the author is taking special care with his or her words, which is certainly important when composing the right answer. After all, there are many ways to be wrong, but there is only one way to be right! For this reason, it is wise to avoid answers that are absolute when taking a multiple-choice test. An absolute answer is one that says things are either all one way or all another. They often include words like *every*, *always*, *best*, and *never*. If you are taking a multiple-choice test in a subject that doesn't lend itself to absolute answers, be on your guard if you see any of these words.

12. Long Answers

In many subject areas, the answers are not simple. As already mentioned, the right answer often requires hedges. Another common feature of the answers to a complex or subjective question are qualifying clauses, which are groups of words that subtly modify the meaning of the sentence. If the question or answer choice describes a rule to which there are exceptions or the subject matter is complicated, ambiguous, or confusing, the correct answer will require many words in order to be expressed clearly and accurately. In essence, you should not be deterred by answer choices that seem excessively long. Oftentimes, the author of the text will not be able to write the correct answer without offering some qualifications and modifications. Your job is to read the answer choices thoroughly and completely and to select the one that most accurately and precisely answers the question.

13. Restating to Understand

Sometimes, a question on a multiple-choice test is difficult not because of what it asks but because of how it is written. If this is the case, restate the question or answer choice in different words. This process serves a couple of important purposes. First, it forces you to concentrate on the core of the question. In order to rephrase the question accurately, you have to understand it well. Rephrasing the question will concentrate your mind on the key words and ideas. Second, it will present the information to your mind in a fresh way. This process may trigger your memory and render some useful scrap of information picked up while studying.

14. True Statements

Sometimes an answer choice will be true in itself, but it does not answer the question. This is one of the main reasons why it is essential to read the question carefully and completely before proceeding to the answer choices. Too often, test takers skip ahead to the answer choices and look for true statements. Having found one of these, they are content to select it without reference to the question above. Obviously, this provides an easy way for test makers to play tricks. The savvy test taker will always read the entire question before turning to the answer choices. Then, having settled on a correct answer choice, he or she will refer to the original question and ensure that the selected answer is relevant. The mistake of choosing a correct-but-irrelevant answer choice is especially common on questions related to specific pieces of objective knowledge. A prepared test taker will have a wealth of factual knowledge at his or her disposal, and should not be careless in its application.

15. No Patterns

One of the more dangerous ideas that circulates about multiple-choice tests is that the correct answers tend to fall into patterns. These erroneous ideas range from a belief that B and C are the most common right answers, to the idea that an unprepared test-taker should answer "A-B-A-C-A-D-A-B-A." It cannot be emphasized enough that pattern-seeking of this type is exactly the WRONG way to approach a multiple-choice test. To begin with, it is highly unlikely that the test maker will plot the correct answers according to some predetermined pattern. The questions are scrambled and delivered in a random order. Furthermore, even if the test maker was following a pattern in the assignation of correct answers, there is no reason why the test taker would know which pattern he or she was using. Any attempt to discern a pattern in the answer choices is a waste of time and a distraction from the real work of taking the test. A test taker would be much better served by extra preparation before the test than by reliance on a pattern in the answers.

FREE DVD OFFER

Don't forget that doing well on your exam includes both understanding the test content and understanding how to use what you know to do well on the test. We offer a completely FREE Test Taking Tips DVD that covers world class test taking tips that you can use to be even more successful when you are taking your test.

All that we ask is that you email us your feedback about your study guide. To get your **FREE Test Taking Tips DVD**, email freedvd@studyguideteam.com with "FREE DVD" in the subject line and the following information in the body of the email:

- The title of your study guide.
- Your product rating on a scale of 1-5, with 5 being the highest rating.
- Your feedback about the study guide. What did you think of it?
- Your full name and shipping address to send your free DVD.

Introduction

Function of the Test

Advanced Placement (AP) Exams are tests given by the College Board across the United States and internationally to determine placement into or credits toward college courses. Usually a score of 3 or higher on an exam will determine if a student receives credit toward a college course, as the scores go from 1 to 5, with 5 being viewed as receiving an "A." The demographics for taking the AP Exam are high school students or those who are interested in going back to college. In 2018, 580,043 people took the AP English Language and Composition Exam.

Test Administration

AP Exams are offered in May of each year and are usually given at the end of an AP course, although taking an AP course prior to the exam is not required. Check with your school to register for the AP Exam. If your school does not offer the AP Exam, the College Board website has information on where exams are located and what to bring on test day. Test takers may not take an AP Exam twice in one year, but they may retake the same exam the following year. Schools will receive the first score and each subsequent score thereafter. Any test takers with disabilities may receive accommodations by submitting a request to the College Board website.

Test Format

The AP English Language and Composition Exam is 3 hours and 15 minutes long and includes multiple-choice and free-response questions. The subjects in this exam include reading comprehension of diverse texts, rhetorical analysis, synthesis of information, and written argumentation. The multiple-choice portion makes up 45% of the exam, and the free-response portion makes up 55% of the exam. Check out the information below on each section:

- Multiple-Choice Section: Up to 55 questions, 1 hour long
- Free-Response Section: 3 response questions, 2 hours and 15 minutes long.

On test day, test takers should bring sharpened No. 2 pencils, pens, a school code, a basic watch, the AP student pack, and an ID. Test takers should not bring electronics, books, scratch paper, earplugs, food, drink, or clipboards.

Scoring

Overall, the AP exam is a weighted combination of scores from the free-response and multiple-choice questions. The free-response questions are scored on a scale of 0 to 9, with 9 being a sophisticated argument and with 0 being an off-topic response. The way the AP Exam will be reported as a whole is in increments of 5 points, which 5 indicating extremely well qualified, 4 indicating well qualified, 3 indicating qualified, 2 indicating possibly qualified, and 1 indicating no recommendation. With AP scores that are qualified, it is possible to earn college credits or advanced placement. Note that incorrect answers will not be penalized, so students should fill in every multiple-choice question, even if they do not know the answer. In 2018, 57.2% of test takers scored a 3 or higher.

Recent/Future Developments

The following are changes made for the 2019-20 AP Exam:

- Analytic Rubrics will be used for the 3 response questions, which gives more specific instruction on Instructional Planning Reports
- Multiple-choice questions will include composition as well as textual analysis.
- Vocabulary in context and identification will no longer be represented in the questions.
- The reading passages will remain consistent in difficulty.
- Reading and composition will be more equally represented on the exam.

Reading Comprehension

Components of a Text

Understanding Authors' Claims

The goal of most persuasive and informative texts is to make a claim and support it with evidence. A **claim** is a statement made as though it is fact. Many claims are opinions; for example, "stealing is wrong." While this is generally true, it is arguable, meaning it is capable of being challenged. An initial reaction to "stealing is wrong" might be to agree; however, there may be circumstances in which it is warranted. If it is necessary for the survival of an individual or their loved ones (i.e., if they are starving and cannot afford to eat), then this assertion becomes morally ambiguous. While it may still be illegal, whether it is "wrong" is unclear.

When an assertion is made within a text, it is typically reinforced with supporting details as is exemplified in the following passage:

> The extinction of the dinosaurs has been a hot debate amongst scientists since the discovery of fossils in the eighteenth century. Numerous theories were developed in explanation, including extreme climate change, an epidemic of disease, or changes in the atmosphere. It wasn't until the late 1970s that a young geochemist, named Walter Alvarez, noticed significant changes in the soil layers of limestone he was studying in Italy. The layers contained fossilized remains of millions of small organisms within the layer that corresponded with the same period in which the dinosaurs lived. He noticed that the soil layer directly above this layer was suddenly devoid of any trace of these organisms. The soil layer directly above *this* layer was filled with an entirely new species of organisms. It seemed the first species had disappeared at the exact same time as the dinosaurs!
>
> With the help of his father, Walter Alvarez analyzed the soil layer between the extinct species and the new species and realized this layer was filled with an abnormal amount of *iridium* – a substance that is abundant in meteorites but almost never found on Earth. Unlike other elements in the fossil record, which take a long time to deposit, the iridium had been laid down very abruptly. The layer also contained high levels of soot, enough to account for all of the earth's forests burning to the ground at the same time. This led scientists to create the best-supported theory that the tiny organisms, as well as the dinosaurs and countless other species, had been destroyed by a giant asteroid that had slammed into Earth, raining tons of iridium down on the planet from a giant cosmic cloud.

<u>Supporting Claims</u>
Before embarking on answering these questions, readers should summarize each. This will help in locating the supporting evidence. These summaries can be written down or completed mentally; full sentences are not necessary.

Paragraph 1: Layer of limestone shows that a species of organisms disappeared at same time as the dinosaurs

Paragraph 2: Layer had high amounts of iridium and soot – scientists believe dinosaurs destroyed by asteroid.

Simply by summarizing the text, it has been plainly outlined where there will be answers to relevant questions. Although there are often claims already embedded within an educational text, a claim will most likely be given, but the evidence to support it will need to be located. Take this example question:

> Q: What evidence within the text best supports the theory that the dinosaurs became extinct because of an asteroid?

The claim here is that the dinosaurs went extinct because of an asteroid. Because the text is already outlined in the summaries, it is easy to see that the evidence supporting this theory is in the second paragraph:

> With the help of his father, they analyzed the soil layer between the extinct species and the new species and realized this layer was filled with an abnormal amount of *iridium* – a substance that is abundant is meteorites but almost never found on Earth. Unlike other elements in the fossil record, which takes a long time to deposit, the iridium had been laid down very abruptly. The layer also contained high levels of soot, enough to account for all of the earth's forests burning to the ground at the same time. This led scientists to create the best-supported theory that the tiny organisms, as well as the dinosaurs and countless other species, had been destroyed by a giant asteroid that had slammed into Earth, raining tons of iridium down on the planet from a giant cosmic cloud.

Now that the evidence within the text that best supports the theory has been located, the answer choices can be evaluated:

a. Changes in climate and atmosphere caused an asteroid to crash into Earth
b. Walter and Luis Alvarez studied limestone with fossilized organisms
c. A soil layer lacking organisms that existed at the same time as the dinosaurs showed low levels of iridium
d. A soil layer lacking organisms that existed at the same time as the dinosaurs showed high levels of iridium

Answer choice (a) is clearly false as there is nothing within the text that claims that climate changes caused an asteroid to crash into Earth. This kind of answer choice displays an incorrect use of detail. Although the passage may have contained the words "change," "climate," and "atmosphere," these terms were manipulated to form an erroneous answer.

Answer choice (b) is incorrect because while the scientists did study limestone with fossilized organisms, and in doing so they discovered evidence that led to the formation of the theory, this is not the actual evidence itself. This is an example of an out-of-scope answer choice: a true statement that may or may not have been in the passage, but that isn't the whole answer or isn't the point.

Answer choice (c) is incorrect because it is the opposite of the correct answer. Assuming the second paragraph was summarized correctly, it is already known that the soil layer contained *high* levels of iridium, not low levels. Even if the paragraph was not summarized that way, the final sentence states that "tons of iridium rained down on the planet." So, answer choice (c) is false.

Answer choice (d) is correct because it matches the evidence found in the second paragraph.

Theme

The **theme** is the central message of a fictional work, whether that work is structured as prose, drama, or poetry. It is the heart of what an author is trying to say to readers through the writing, and theme is largely conveyed through literary elements and techniques.

In literature, a theme can often be determined by considering the over-arching narrative conflict within the work. Though there are several types of conflicts and several potential themes within them, the following are the most common:

- **Individual against the self**—relevant to themes of self-awareness, internal struggles, pride, coming of age, facing reality, fate, free will, vanity, loss of innocence, loneliness, isolation, fulfillment, failure, and disillusionment
- **Individual against nature**—relevant to themes of knowledge vs. ignorance, nature as beauty, quest for discovery, self-preservation, chaos and order, circle of life, death, and destruction of beauty
- **Individual against society**—relevant to themes of power, beauty, good, evil, war, class struggle, totalitarianism, role of men/women, wealth, corruption, change vs. tradition, capitalism, destruction, heroism, injustice, and racism
- **Individual against another individual**—relevant to themes of hope, loss of love or hope, sacrifice, power, revenge, betrayal, and honor

For example, in Hawthorne's *The Scarlet Letter*, one possible narrative conflict could be the individual against the self, with a relevant theme of internal struggles. This theme is alluded to through characterization—Dimmesdale's moral struggle with his love for Hester and Hester's internal struggles with the truth and her daughter, Pearl. It's also alluded to through plot—Dimmesdale's suicide and Hester helping the very townspeople who initially condemned her.

Sometimes, a text can convey a **message** or **universal lesson**—a truth or insight that the reader infers from the text, based on analysis of the literary and/or poetic elements. This message is often presented as a statement. For example, a potential message in Shakespeare's *Hamlet* could be "Revenge is what ultimately drives the human soul." This message can be immediately determined through plot and characterization in numerous ways, but it can also be determined through the setting of Norway, which is bordering on war.

<u>How Authors Develop Theme</u>
Authors employ a variety of techniques to present a theme. They may compare or contrast characters, events, places, ideas, or historical or invented settings to speak thematically. They may use analogies, metaphors, similes, allusions, or other literary devices to convey the theme. An author's use of diction, syntax, and tone can also help convey the theme. Authors will often develop themes through the development of characters, use of the setting, repetition of ideas, use of symbols, and through

contrasting value systems. Authors of both fiction and nonfiction genres will use a variety of these techniques to develop one or more themes.

Regardless of the literary genre, there are commonalities in how authors, playwrights, and poets develop themes or central ideas.

Authors often do research, the results of which contributes to theme. In prose fiction and drama, this research may include real historical information about the setting the author has chosen or include elements that make fictional characters, settings, and plots seem realistic to the reader. In nonfiction, research is critical since the information contained within this literature must be accurate and, moreover, accurately represented.

In fiction, authors present a narrative conflict that will contribute to the overall theme. In fiction, this conflict may involve the storyline itself and some trouble within characters that needs resolution. In nonfiction, this conflict may be an explanation or commentary on factual people and events.

Authors will sometimes use character motivation to convey theme, such as in the example from *Hamlet* regarding revenge. In fiction, the characters an author creates will think, speak, and act in ways that effectively convey the theme to readers. In nonfiction, the characters are factual, as in a biography, but authors pay particular attention to presenting those motivations to make them clear to readers.

Authors also use literary devices as a means of conveying theme. For example, the use of moon symbolism in Mary Shelley's *Frankenstein* is significant as its phases can be compared to the phases that the Creature undergoes as he struggles with his identity.

The selected point of view can also contribute to a work's theme. The use of first-person point of view in a fiction or non-fiction work engages the reader's response differently than third person point of view. The central idea or theme from a first-person narrative may differ from a third-person limited text.

In literary nonfiction, authors usually identify the purpose of their writing, which differs from fiction, where the general purpose is to entertain. The purpose of nonfiction is usually to inform, persuade, or entertain the audience. The stated purpose of a non-fiction text will drive how the central message or theme, if applicable, is presented.

Authors identify an audience for their writing, which is critical in shaping the theme of the work. For example, the audience for J.K. Rowling's *Harry Potter* series would be different than the audience for a biography of George Washington. The audience an author chooses to address is closely tied to the purpose of the work. The choice of an audience also drives the choice of language and level of diction an author uses. Ultimately, the intended audience determines the level to which that subject matter is presented and the complexity of the theme.

<u>Cultural Influence on Themes</u>

Regardless of culture, place, or time, certain themes are universal to the human condition. Because all humans experience certain feelings and engage in similar experiences—birth, death, marriage, friendship, finding meaning, etc.—certain themes span cultures. However, different cultures have different norms and general beliefs concerning these themes. For example, the theme of maturing and crossing from childhood to adulthood is a global theme; however, the literature from one culture might imply that this happens in someone's twenties, while another culture's literature might imply that it happens in the early teenage years.

It's important for the reader to be aware of these differences. Readers must avoid being *ethnocentric*, which means believing the aspects of one's own culture to be superior to that of other cultures.

Author's Purpose

No matter the genre or format, all authors are writing to persuade, inform, entertain, or express feelings. Often, these purposes are blended, with one dominating the rest. It's useful to learn to recognize the author's intent.

Persuasive writing is used to persuade or convince readers of something. It often contains two elements: the argument and the counterargument. The argument takes a stance on an issue, while the counterargument pokes holes in the opposition's stance. Authors rely on logic, emotion, and writer credibility to persuade readers to agree with them. If readers are opposed to the stance before reading, they are unlikely to adopt that stance. However, those who are undecided or committed to the same stance are more likely to agree with the author.

Informative writing tries to teach or inform. Workplace manuals, instructor lessons, statistical reports and cookbooks are examples of informative texts. Informative writing is usually based on facts and is often void of emotion and persuasion. Informative texts generally contain statistics, charts, and graphs. Though most informative texts lack a persuasive agenda, readers must examine the text carefully to determine whether one exists within a given passage.

Stories or narratives are designed to entertain. When you go to the movies, you often want to escape for a few hours, not necessarily to think critically. Entertaining writing is designed to delight and engage the reader. However, sometimes this type of writing can be woven into more serious materials, such as persuasive or informative writing to hook the reader before transitioning into a more scholarly discussion.

Emotional writing works to evoke the reader's feelings, such as anger, euphoria, or sadness. The connection between reader and author is an attempt to cause the reader to share the author's intended emotion or tone. Sometimes in order to make a piece more poignant, the author simply wants readers to feel the same emotions that the author has felt. Other times, the author attempts to persuade or manipulate the reader into adopting his stance. While it's okay to sympathize with the author, be aware of the individual's underlying intent.

Author's Position

When it comes to authors' writings, readers should always identify a position or stance. No matter how objective a piece may seem, assume the author has preconceived beliefs. Reduce the likelihood of accepting an invalid argument by looking for multiple articles on the topic, including those with varying opinions. If several opinions point in the same direction, and are backed by reputable peer-reviewed sources, it's more likely the author has a valid argument. Positions that run contrary to widely held beliefs and existing data should invite scrutiny. There are exceptions to the rule, so be a careful consumer of information.

Though themes, symbols, and motifs are buried deep within the text and can sometimes be difficult to infer, an author's purpose is usually obvious from the beginning. There are four purposes of writing: to inform, to persuade, to describe, and to entertain. Informative writings present facts in an accessible way. Persuasive writing appeals to emotions and logic to inspire the reader to adopt a specific stance. Be wary of this type of writing, as it often lacks objectivity. Descriptive writing is designed to paint a picture in the reader's mind, while writings that entertain are often narratives designed to engage and delight the reader.

The various writing styles are usually blended, with one purpose dominating the rest. For example, a persuasive piece might begin with a humorous tale to make readers more receptive to the persuasive message, or a recipe in a cookbook designed to inform might be preceded by an entertaining anecdote that makes the recipe more appealing.

Author's Style, Tone, and Mood

Style, tone, and mood are often thought to be the same thing. Though they're closely related, there are important differences to keep in mind. The easiest way to do this is to remember that style creates and affects tone and mood. More specifically, style is *how the writer uses words* to create the desired tone and mood for his or her writing.

Style

Style can include any number of technical writing choices, and some may have to be analyzed on the test. A few examples of style choices include:

- **Sentence Construction**: When presenting facts, does the writer use shorter sentences to create a quicker sense of the supporting evidence, or does he or she use longer sentences to elaborate and explain the information?

- **Technical Language**: Does the writer use jargon to demonstrate his or her expertise in the subject, or does he or she use ordinary language to help the reader understand things in simple terms?

- **Formal Language**: Does the writer refrain from using contractions such as *won't* or *can't* to create a more formal tone, or does he or she use a colloquial, conversational style to connect to the reader?

- **Formatting**: Does the writer use a series of shorter paragraphs to help the reader follow a line of argument, or does he or she use longer paragraphs to examine an issue in great detail and demonstrate their knowledge of the topic?

On the test, examine the writer's style and how their writing choices affect the way the text comes across.

Tone

Tone refers to the writer's attitude toward the subject matter. For example, the tone conveys how the writer feels about the topic he or she is writing about. A lot of nonfiction writing has a neutral tone, which is an important tone for the writer to take. A neutral tone demonstrates that the writer is presenting a topic impartially and letting the information speak for itself. On the other hand, nonfiction writing can be just as effective and appropriate if the tone isn't neutral. For instance, consider this example:

> Seat belts save more lives than any other automobile safety feature. Many studies show that airbags save lives as well; however, not all cars have airbags. For instance, some older cars don't. Furthermore, air bags aren't entirely reliable. For example, studies show that in 15% of accidents, airbags don't deploy as designed; but, on the other hand, seat belt malfunctions are extremely rare. The number of highway fatalities has plummeted since laws requiring seat belt usage were enacted.

In this passage, the writer mostly chooses to retain a neutral tone when presenting information. If the writer would instead include their own personal experience of losing a friend or family member in a car accident, the tone would change dramatically. The tone would no longer be neutral and would show that the writer has a personal stake in the content, allowing them to interpret the information in a different way. When analyzing tone, consider what the writer is trying to achieve in the text and how they *create* the tone using style.

Mood

Mood refers to the feelings and atmosphere that the writer's words create for the reader. Like tone, many nonfiction texts can have a neutral mood. To return to the previous example, if the writer chose to include information about a person they knew dying in a car accident, the text would carry an emotional component that is absent in the previous example. Depending on how they present the information, the writer can create a sad, angry, or even hopeful mood. When analyzing the mood, consider what the writer wants to accomplish and whether the best choice was made to achieve that end.

Rhetorical Strategies

Rhetorical Appeals

In nonfiction writing, authors employ argumentative techniques to present their opinion to readers in the most convincing way. First of all, persuasive writing usually includes at least one type of appeal: an appeal to logic (**logos**), emotion (**pathos**), or credibility and trustworthiness (**ethos**). When a writer appeals to logic, they are asking readers to agree with them based on research, evidence, and an established line of reasoning. An author's argument might also appeal to readers' emotions, perhaps by including personal stories and anecdotes (a short narrative of a specific event). A final type of appeal—appeal to authority—asks the reader to agree with the author's argument on the basis of their expertise or credentials. Consider three different approaches to arguing the same opinion:

Logic (Logos)
Below is an example of an appeal to logic. The author uses evidence to disprove the logic of the school's rule (the rule was supposed to reduce discipline problems; the number of problems has not been reduced; therefore, the rule is not working) and he or she calls for its repeal.

> Our school should abolish its current ban on cell phone use on campus. This rule was adopted last year as an attempt to reduce class disruptions and help students focus more on their lessons. However, since the rule was enacted, there has been no change in the number of disciplinary problems in class. Therefore, the rule is ineffective and should be done away with.

Emotion (Pathos)
An author's argument might also appeal to readers' emotions, perhaps by including personal stories and anecdotes. The next example presents an appeal to emotion. By sharing the personal anecdote of one student and speaking about emotional topics like family relationships, the author invokes the reader's empathy in asking them to reconsider the school rule.

> Our school should abolish its current ban on cell phone use on campus. If they aren't able to use their phones during the school day, many students feel isolated from their loved ones. For example, last semester, one student's grandmother had a heart attack in the morning. However, because he couldn't use his cell phone, the student didn't know about his grandmother's condition until the end of the day—when she had already passed away and it was too late to say goodbye. By preventing students from contacting their friends and family, our school is placing undue stress and anxiety on students.

Credibility (Ethos)
Finally, an appeal to authority includes a statement from a relevant expert. In this case, the author uses a doctor in the field of education to support the argument. All three examples begin from the same opinion—the school's phone ban needs to change—but rely on different argumentative styles to persuade the reader.

> Our school should abolish its current ban on cell phone use on campus. According to Dr. Bartholomew Everett, a leading educational expert, "Research studies show that cell phone usage has no real impact on student attentiveness. Rather, phones provide a valuable technological resource for learning. Schools need to learn how to integrate this new technology into their curriculum." Rather than banning phones altogether, our school should follow the advice of experts and allow students to use phones as part of their learning.

Rhetorical Questions
Another commonly used argumentative technique is asking **rhetorical questions**, questions that do not actually require an answer but that push the reader to consider the topic further.

> I wholly disagree with the proposal to ban restaurants from serving foods with high sugar and sodium contents. Do we really want to live in a world where the government can control what we eat? I prefer to make my own food choices.

Here, the author's rhetorical question prompts readers to put themselves in a hypothetical situation and imagine how they would feel about it.

Figurative Language

Similes and **metaphors** are part of figurative language that are used as rhetorical devices. Both are comparisons between two things, but their formats differ slightly. A simile says that two things are similar and makes a comparison using "like" or "as"—*A* is like *B,* or *A* is as [some characteristic] as *B*—whereas a metaphor states that two things are exactly the same—*A* is *B*. In both cases, similes and metaphors invite the reader to think more deeply about the characteristics of the two subjects and consider where they overlap. Sometimes the poet develops a complex metaphor throughout the entire poem; this is known as an extended metaphor. An example of metaphor can be found in the sentence: "His pillow was a fluffy cloud". An example of simile can be found in the first line of Robert Burns' famous poem:

> My love is like a red, red rose

This is comparison using "like," and the two things being compared are love and a rose. Some characteristics of a rose are that it is fragrant, beautiful, blossoming, colorful, vibrant—by comparing his love to a red, red rose, Burns asks the reader to apply these qualities of a rose to his love. In this way, he implies that his love is also fresh, blossoming, and brilliant.

In addition to rhetorical devices that play on the *meanings* of words, there are also rhetorical devices that use the sounds of words. These devices are most often found in poetry, but may also be found in other types of literature and in nonfiction writing like texts for speeches.

Alliteration and **assonance** are both varieties of sound repetition. Other types of sound repetition include: **anaphora**—repetition that occurs at the beginning of the sentences; **epiphora**—repetition occurring at the end of phrases; antimetabole—repetition of words in a succession; and antiphrasis—a form of denial of an assertion in a text.

Alliteration refers to the repetition of the first sound of each word. Recall Robert Burns' opening line:

> My love is like a red, red rose

This line includes two instances of alliteration: "love" and "like" (repeated *L* sound), as well as "red" and "rose" (repeated *R* sound). Next, assonance refers to the repetition of vowel sounds, and can occur anywhere within a word (not just the opening sound). Here is the opening of a poem by John Keats:

> When I have fears that I may cease to be
>
> Before my pen has glean'd my teeming brain

Assonance can be found in the words "fears," "cease," "be," "glean'd," and "teeming," all of which stress the long *E* sound. Both alliteration and assonance create a harmony that unifies the writer's language.

Another sound device is **onomatopoeia**—words whose spelling mimics the sound they describe. Words such as "crash," "bang," and "sizzle" are all examples of onomatopoeia. Use of onomatopoetic language adds auditory imagery to the text.

Readers are probably most familiar with the technique of using a **pun**. A pun is a play on words, taking advantage of two words that have the same or similar pronunciation. Puns can be found throughout Shakespeare's plays, for instance:

> Now is the winter of our discontent
>
> Made glorious summer by this son of York

These lines from *Richard III* contain a play on words. Richard III refers to his brother—the newly crowned King Edward IV—as the "son of York," referencing their family heritage from the house of York. However, while drawing a comparison between the political climate and the weather (times of political trouble were the "winter," but now the new king brings "glorious summer"), Richard's use of the word "son" also implies another word with the same pronunciation, "sun"—so Edward IV is also like the sun, bringing light, warmth, and hope to England. Puns are a clever way for writers to suggest two meanings at once.

Point of View

Point of view is another important writing device to consider. In fiction writing, **point of view** refers to who tells the story or from whose perspective readers are observing as they read. In nonfiction writing, the **point of view** refers to whether the author refers to himself or herself, his or her readers, or chooses not to mention either. Whether fiction or nonfiction, the author carefully considers the impact the perspective will have on the purpose and main point of the writing.

- **First-person** point of view: The story is told from the writer's perspective. In fiction, this would mean that the main character is also the narrator. First-person point of view is easily recognized by the use of personal pronouns such as *I, me, we, us, our, my*, and *myself*.
- **Third-person** point of view: In a more formal essay, this would be an appropriate perspective because the focus should be on the subject matter, not the writer or the reader. Third-person point of view is recognized by the use of the pronouns *he, she, they*, and *it*. In fiction writing, third person point of view has a few variations.
    - ***Third-person limited*** point of view refers to a story told by a narrator who has access to the thoughts and feelings of just one character.
    - In **third-person omniscient** point of view, the narrator has access to the thoughts and feelings of all the characters.
    - In **third-person objective** point of view, the narrator is like a fly on the wall and can see and hear what the characters do and say but does not have access to their thoughts and feelings.

- **Second-person** point of view: This point of view isn't commonly used in fiction or nonfiction writing because it directly addresses the reader using the pronouns *you, your*, and *yourself*. Second-person perspective is more appropriate in direct communication, such as business letters or emails.

Point of View	Pronouns used
First person	I, me, we, us, our, my, myself
Second person	You, your, yourself
Third person	He, she, it, they

Types of Passages

Writing can be classified under four passage types: narrative, expository, descriptive (sometimes called technical), and persuasive. Though these types are not mutually exclusive, one form tends to dominate the rest. By recognizing the type of passage you're reading, you gain insight into how you should read. If you're reading a narrative, you can assume the author intends to entertain, which means you may skim the text without losing meaning. A technical document might require a close read, because skimming the passage might cause the reader to miss salient details.

1. **Narrative writing**, at its core, is the art of storytelling. For a narrative to exist, certain elements must be present. First, it must have characters. While many characters are human, characters could be defined as anything that thinks, acts, and talks like a human. For example, many recent movies, such as *Lord of the Rings* and *The Chronicles of Narnia*, include animals, fantastical creatures, and even trees that behave like humans. Second, it must have a plot or sequence of events. Typically, those events follow a standard plot diagram, but recent trends start *in medias res* or in the middle (near the climax). In this instance, foreshadowing and flashbacks often fill in plot details. Finally, along with characters and a plot, there must also be conflict. Conflict is usually divided into two types: internal and external. Internal conflict indicates the character is in turmoil and is presented through the character's thoughts. External conflicts are visible. Types of external conflict include a person versus nature, another person, or society.

2. **Expository writing** is detached and to the point. Since expository writing is designed to instruct or inform, it usually involves directions and steps written in second person ("you" voice) and lacks any persuasive or narrative elements. Sequence words such as *first, second*, and *third*, or *in the first place, secondly*, and *lastly* are often given to add fluency and cohesion. Common examples of expository writing include instructor's lessons, cookbook recipes, and repair manuals.

3. Due to its empirical nature, **technical writing** is filled with steps, charts, graphs, data, and statistics. The goal of technical writing is to advance understanding in a field through the scientific method. Experts such as teachers, doctors, or mechanics use words unique to the profession in which they operate. These words, which often incorporate acronyms, are called *jargon*. Technical writing is a type of expository writing but is not meant to be understood by the general public. Instead, technical writers assume readers have received a formal education in a particular field of study and need no explanation as to what the jargon means. Imagine a doctor trying to understand a diagnostic reading for a car or a mechanic trying to interpret lab results. Only professionals with proper training will fully comprehend the text.

4. **Persuasive writing** is designed to change opinions and attitudes. The topic, stance, and arguments are found in the thesis, positioned near the end of the introduction. Later supporting paragraphs offer

relevant quotations, paraphrases, and summaries from primary or secondary sources, which are then interpreted, analyzed, and evaluated. The goal of persuasive writers is not to stack quotes, but to develop original ideas by using sources as a starting point. Good persuasive writing makes powerful arguments with valid sources and thoughtful analysis. Poor persuasive writing is riddled with bias and logical fallacies. Sometimes logical and illogical arguments are sandwiched together in the same piece. Therefore, readers should display skepticism when reading persuasive arguments.

Passage Development

Transition Words

The writer should act as a guide, showing the reader how all the sentences fit together. Consider this example:

> Seat belts save more lives than any other automobile safety feature. Many studies show that airbags save lives as well. Not all cars have airbags. Many older cars don't. Air bags aren't entirely reliable. Studies show that in 15% of accidents, airbags don't deploy as designed. Seat belt malfunctions are extremely rare.

There's nothing wrong with any of these sentences individually, but together they're disjointed and difficult to follow. The best way for the writer to communicate information is through the use of transition words. Here are examples of transition words and phrases that tie sentences together, enabling a more natural flow:

- To show causality: *as a result*, *therefore*, and *consequently*
- To compare and contrast: *however*, *but*, and *on the other hand*
- To introduce examples*: for instance*, *namely*, and *including*
- To show order of importance: *foremost*, *primarily*, *secondly*, and *lastly*

NOTE: This is not a complete list of transitions. There are many more that can be used; however, most fit into these or similar categories. The point is that the words should clearly show the relationship between sentences, supporting information, and the main idea.

Here is an update to the previous example using transition words. These changes make it easier to read and bring clarity to the writer's points:

> Seat belts save more lives than any other automobile safety feature. Many studies show that airbags save lives as well; however, not all cars have airbags. For instance, some older cars don't. Furthermore, air bags aren't entirely reliable. For example, studies show that in 15% of accidents, airbags don't deploy as designed; but, on the other hand, seat belt malfunctions are extremely rare.

Also, be prepared to analyze whether the writer is using the best transition word or phrase for the situation. Take this sentence for example: "As a result, seat belt malfunctions are extremely rare." This sentence doesn't make sense in the context above because the writer is trying to show the contrast between seat belts and airbags, not the causality.

Logical Sequence

Even if the writer includes plenty of information to support their point, the writing is only coherent when the information is in a logical order. **Logical sequencing** is really just common sense, but it's an important writing technique. First, the writer should introduce the main idea, whether for a paragraph, a section, or the entire piece. Second, they should present evidence to support the main idea by using transitional language. This shows the reader how the information relates to the main idea and the sentences around it. The writer should then take time to interpret the information, making sure necessary connections are obvious to the reader. Finally, the writer can summarize the information in a closing section.

NOTE: Though most writing follows this pattern, it isn't a set rule. Sometimes writers change the order for effect. For example, the writer can begin with a surprising piece of supporting information to grab the reader's attention, and then transition to the main idea. Thus, if a passage doesn't follow the logical order, don't immediately assume it's wrong. However, most writing usually settles into a logical sequence after a nontraditional beginning.

<u>Introductions and Conclusions</u>

Examining the writer's strategies for introductions and conclusions puts the reader in the right mindset to interpret the rest of the text. Look for methods the writer might use for **introductions** such as:

- Stating the main point immediately, followed by outlining how the rest of the piece supports this claim.
- Establishing important, smaller pieces of the main idea first, and then grouping these points into a case for the main idea.
- Opening with a quotation, anecdote, question, seeming paradox, or other piece of interesting information, and then using it to lead to the main point.
- Whatever method the writer chooses, the introduction should make their intention clear, establish their voice as a credible one, and encourage a person to continue reading.

Conclusions tend to follow a similar pattern. In them, the writer restates their main idea a final time, often after summarizing the smaller pieces of that idea. If the introduction uses a quote or anecdote to grab the reader's attention, the conclusion often makes reference to it again. Whatever way the writer chooses to arrange the conclusion, the final restatement of the main idea should be clear and simple for the reader to interpret. Finally, conclusions shouldn't introduce any new information.

Analyzing Text Structure

<u>Organizational Structure within Literary Texts</u>

Depending on what the author is attempting to accomplish, certain formats or text structures work better than others. For example, a sequence structure might work for narration but not when identifying similarities and differences between dissimilar concepts. Similarly, a comparison-contrast structure is not useful for narration. It's the author's job to put the right information in the correct format.

Readers should be familiar with the five main literary structures:

1. **Sequence** structure (sometimes referred to as the order structure) is when the order of events proceeds in a predictable manner. In many cases, this means the text goes through the plot elements: exposition, rising action, climax, falling action, and resolution. Readers are introduced to characters, setting, and conflict in the exposition. In the rising action, there's an increase in tension and suspense. The climax is the height of tension and the point of no return. Tension decreases

during the falling action. In the resolution, any conflicts presented in the exposition are solved, and the story concludes. An informative text that is structured sequentially will often go in order from one step to the next.

2. In the **problem-solution** structure, authors identify a potential problem and suggest a solution. This form of writing is usually divided into two paragraphs and can be found in informational texts. For example, cell phone, cable, and satellite providers use this structure in manuals to help customers troubleshoot or identify problems with services or products.

3. When authors want to discuss similarities and differences between separate concepts, they arrange thoughts in a **comparison-contrast** paragraph structure. **Venn diagrams** are an effective graphic organizer for comparison-contrast structures, because they feature two overlapping circles that can be used to organize and group similarities and differences. A comparison-contrast essay organizes one paragraph based on similarities and another based on differences. A comparison-contrast essay can also be arranged with the similarities and differences of individual traits addressed within individual paragraphs. Words such as *however*, *but*, and *nevertheless* help signal a contrast in ideas.

4. The **descriptive** writing structure is designed to appeal to one's senses. Much like an artist who constructs a painting, good descriptive writing builds an image in the reader's mind by appealing to the five senses: sight, hearing, taste, touch, and smell. However, overly descriptive writing can become tedious; sparse descriptions can make settings and characters seem flat. Good authors strike a balance by applying descriptions only to passages, characters, and settings that are integral to the plot.

5. Passages that use the **cause and effect** structure are simply asking *why* by demonstrating some type of connection between ideas. Words such as *if*, *since*, *because*, *then*, or *consequently* indicate relationship. By switching the order of a complex sentence, the writer can rearrange the emphasis on different clauses. Saying *If Sheryl is late, we'll miss the dance* is different from saying, *We'll miss the dance if Sheryl is late*. One emphasizes Sheryl's tardiness while the other emphasizes missing the dance. Paragraphs can also be arranged in a cause and effect format. Since the format—before and after—is sequential, it is useful when authors wish to discuss the impact of choices. Researchers often apply this paragraph structure to the scientific method.

<u>Organizational Structure within Informational Texts</u>

Informational text is specifically designed to relate factual information, and although it is open to a reader's interpretation and application of the facts, the structure of the presentation is carefully designed to lead the reader to a particular conclusion or central idea. When reading informational text, it is important that readers are able to understand its organizational structure as the structure often directly relates to an author's intent to inform and/or persuade the reader.

The first step in identifying the text's structure is to determine the thesis or main idea. The thesis statement and organization of a work are closely intertwined. A **thesis statement** indicates the writer's purpose and may include the scope and direction of the text. It may be presented at the beginning of a text or at the end, and it may be explicit or implicit.

Once a reader has a grasp of the thesis or main idea of the text, he or she can better determine its organizational structure. Test takers are advised to read informational text passages more than once in order to comprehend the material fully. It is also helpful to examine any text features present in the text including the table of contents, index, glossary, headings, footnotes, and visuals. The analysis of these features and the information presented within them, can offer additional clues about the central idea and structure of a text. The following questions should be asked when considering structure:

- How does the author assemble the parts to make an effective whole argument?
- Is the passage linear in nature and if so, what is the timeline or thread of logic?
- What is the presented order of events, facts, or arguments? Are these effective in contributing to the author's thesis?
- How can the passage be divided into sections? How are they related to each other and to the main idea or thesis?
- What key terms are used to indicate the organization?

Next, test takers should skim the passage, noting the first line or two of each body paragraph—the **topic sentences**—and the conclusion. Key **transitional terms**, such as *on the other hand*, *also*, *because*, *however*, *therefore*, *most importantly*, and *first*, within the text can also signal organizational structure. Based on these clues, readers should then be able to identify what type of organizational structure is being used.

The following organizational structures are most common:

- **Problem/solution**—organized by an analysis/overview of a problem, followed by potential solution(s)

- **Cause/effect**—organized by the effects resulting from a cause or the cause(s) of a particular effect

- **Spatial order**—organized by points that suggest location or direction—e.g., top to bottom, right to left, outside to inside

- **Chronological/sequence order**—organized by points presented to indicate a passage of time or through purposeful steps/stages

- **Comparison/Contrast**—organized by points that indicate similarities and/or differences between two things or concepts

- **Order of importance**—organized by priority of points, often most significant to least significant or vice versa

Context Clues

Knowledge of synonyms and antonyms is crucial for writing and identifying a good paraphrase and also helps readers expand their mental vocabulary network. Another useful vocabulary skill is being able to understand meaning in context. A word's **context** refers to all the other words and information surrounding it, and the context of a word can have an impact on how readers interpret that word's meaning. Of course, many words have more than one definition. For example, consider the meaning of the word *engaged*.

The first definition that comes to mind might be "promised to be married," but consider the following sentences:

A: The two armies engaged in a conflict that lasted all night.

B: The three-hour lecture flew by because students were so engaged in the material.

C: The busy executive engaged a new assistant to help with his workload.

As you can see, *engaged* has a variety of other meanings. In these sentences, respectively, it can mean: "battled," "interested or involved," and "appointed or employed." With so many possible definitions, readers may wonder how to decide which one to apply in a given sentence. The appropriate meaning is prioritized based on context. For example, sentence *C* mentions "executive," "assistant," and "workload," so readers can assume that *engaged* has something to do with work—in which case, "appointed or employed" would be the best definition for this context. Context clues can also be found in sentence *A*. Words like "armies" and "conflicts" show that this sentence is about a military situation (and not about marriage or the office), so in this context, *engaged* is closest in meaning to "battled." By using context clues—the surrounding words in the sentence—readers can easily select the most appropriate definition for the word in question.

In addition to helping readers select the best meaning for a word with many definitions, context clues can also help readers when they don't know any meanings for a certain word. Test writers will deliberately ask about vocabulary that test takers are probably unfamiliar with in order to measure their ability to use context to make an educated guess about a word's meaning.

Which of the following is the closest in meaning to the word *loquacious* in the following sentence?

The loquacious professor was notorious for always taking too long to finish his lectures.

a. Knowledgeable
b. Enthusiastic
c. Approachable
d. Talkative
e. Inexperienced

Even if the word *loquacious* seems completely new, it is still possible to utilize context to make a good guess about the word's meaning. Grammatically, it is apparent that *loquacious* is an adjective that modifies the noun "professor"—so *loquacious* must be some kind of quality or characteristic. A clue in this sentence is "taking too long to finish his lectures." Readers should then brainstorm qualities that might cause a professor to be late. Perhaps he is "disorganized," "slow," or "talkative"—all words that might still make sense in this sentence. After brainstorming some ideas for the word's definition, take a look at the choices for the question. Choice *D* matches one word from the brainstorming session, and it is a logical choice for this sentence—the professor talks too much, so his lectures run late. In fact, *loquacious* means "talkative" or "wordy."

One way to use context clues is to think of potential replacement words before considering the answer choices given in the question. However, if it is truly a struggle to come up with any possibilities, turn to the answer choices first and try to replace each of them in the sentence to see if the sentence is still logical and retains the same meaning.

Which of the following is the closest in meaning to the word *dogma* in the following sentence?

Martin Luther was a revolutionary religious figure because he argued against Catholic dogma and encouraged a new interpretation of Christianity.

a. Punishments
b. Doctrines
c. Leadership
d. Procedures
e. History

Based on context, this sentence has something to do with religious conflict and interpretations of Christian faith. The only word related to religious belief is Choice *B*, *doctrines*, which is in fact the best synonym for *dogma*.

Yet another way to use context clues is to consider clues in the word itself. Most students are probably familiar with prefixes, suffixes, and root words—the building blocks of many English words. A little knowledge goes a long way when it comes to these components of English vocabulary, and they can point readers in the right direction when they need help finding an appropriate definition.

Which of the following is the closest in meaning to the word *antipathy* in the following sentence?

A strong antipathy existed between Margaret and her new neighbor, Susan.

a. Enmity
b. Resemblance
c. Relationship
d. Alliance
e. Persuasion

In this case, the sentence does not provide much context for the word *antipathy*. However, the word itself gives some useful clues. The prefix *anti-* means "opposite or against," so *antipathy* probably has a negative meaning. Also, if readers already know words like "sympathy" or "empathy," they might guess that the root word "path" is related to emotions. So, *antipathy* must be a feeling *against* something. *Alliance* is a positive connection, *relationship* is too neutral, and *resemblance* means two things are similar to each other. *Persuasion* usually relates to a set of beliefs or the act of coercing someone of something, so this choice is nonsensical for the provided sentences. The only word that shows a negative or opposite feeling is Choice *A*, *enmity (the feeling of being enemies).* In this way, even an unfamiliar word may contain clues that can indicate its meaning.

Fact and Opinion, Biases, and Stereotypes

It is important to distinguish between facts and opinions when reading a piece of writing. When an author presents **facts**, such as statistics or data, readers should be able to check those facts to verify that they are accurate. When authors share their own thoughts and feelings about a subject, they are expressing their **opinions**.

Authors often use words like *think, feel, believe,* or *in my opinion* when expressing an opinion, but these words won't always appear in an opinion piece, especially if it is formally written. An author's opinion may be backed up by facts, which gives it more credibility, but that opinion should not be taken as fact.

A critical reader should be suspect of an author's opinion, especially if it is only supported by other opinions.

Fact	Opinion
There are nine innings in a game of baseball.	Baseball games run too long.
James Garfield was assassinated on July 2, 1881.	James Garfield was a good president.
McDonald's® has stores in 118 countries.	McDonald's® has the best hamburgers.

Critical readers examine the facts used to support an author's argument. They check the facts against other sources to be sure those facts are correct. They also check the validity of the sources used to be sure those sources are credible, academic, and/or peer-reviewed. When an author uses another person's opinion to support his or her argument, even if it is an expert's opinion, it is still only an opinion and should not be taken as fact. A strong argument uses valid, measurable facts to support ideas. Even then, the reader may disagree with the argument.

An authoritative argument may use the facts to sway the reader. In the example of global warming, many experts differ in their opinions of which alternative fuels can be used to aid in offsetting it. Because of this, a writer may choose to only use the information and experts' opinions that supports his or her viewpoint. For example, if the argument is that wind energy is the best solution, the author will use facts that support this idea. That same author may leave out relevant facts on solar energy. The way the author uses facts can influence the reader, so it's important to consider the facts being used, how those facts are being presented, and what information might be left out.

Authors can also demonstrate **bias** if they ignore an opposing viewpoint or present their side in an unbalanced way. A strong argument considers the opposition and finds a way to refute it. Critical readers should look for an unfair or one-sided presentation of the argument and be skeptical, as a bias may be present. Even if this bias is unintentional, if it exists in the writing, the reader should be wary of the validity of the argument.

Readers should also look for the use of stereotypes that refer to specific groups. **Stereotypes** are often negative connotations about a person or place and should always be avoided. When a critical reader finds stereotypes in a piece of writing, he or she should immediately be critical of the argument and consider the validity of anything the author presents. Stereotypes reveal a flaw in the writer's thinking and may suggest a lack of knowledge or understanding about the subject.

Word Meanings

Connotation refers to the implied meaning of a word or phrase. Connotations are the ideas or feelings that words or phrases invoke other than their literal meaning. An example of the use of connotation is in people's use of the word *cheap*. While the literal meaning is something of low cost, people use the word to suggest something is poor in value or to negatively describe a person as reluctant to spend money. When something or someone is described this way, the reader is more inclined to have a particular image or feeling about it or him/her. Thus, connotation can be a very effective language tool in creating emotion and swaying opinion. However, connotations are sometimes hard to pin down because varying emotions can be associated with a word. Generally, though, connotative meanings tend to be fairly consistent within a specific cultural group.

Denotation is the literal definition of a word or phrase. The denotative meaning of a word is the one you would find in a dictionary. To present hard facts or vocabulary terms, it is helpful for a writer to use words which are mainly known for their denotative meanings rather than their connotative ones. In those instances, the words *inexpensive* and *frugal* are better because they do not carry the negative connotations that cheap does. *Inexpensive* refers to the cost of something, not its value, and *frugal* indicates that a person is conscientiously watching his or her spending. These terms do not elicit the same emotions that *cheap* does.

Authors sometimes choose to use both, but what they choose and when they use it is what critical readers need to differentiate. One method isn't inherently better than the other; however, one may create a better effect, depending upon an author's intent. If, for example, an author's purpose is to inform, to instruct, and to familiarize readers with a difficult subject, his or her use of connotation may be helpful. However, it may also undermine credibility and confuse readers. An author who wants to create a credible, scholarly effect in his or her text would most likely use denotation, which emphasizes literal, factual meaning and examples.

Use a dictionary to find the denotative meaning of words. Though context clues provide a rudimentary understanding of a word, using a dictionary can provide the reader with a more comprehensive meaning of the word. Printed dictionaries list words in alphabetical order, and all versions, including those online, include a word's multiples meanings. Typically, the first definition is the most widely used or known. The second, third, and subsequent entries move toward the more unusual or archaic. Dictionaries also indicate the part of speech of each word, such as noun, verb, adjective, etc.

Keep in mind that dictionaries are not fixed in time. The English language today looks nothing like it did in Shakespeare's time, and Shakespeare's English is vastly different from Chaucer's. The English language is constantly evolving, as evidenced by the deletion of old words and the addition of new. *Ginormous* and *bling-bling*, for example, can both be found in *Merriam-Webster's* latest edition.

Word Parts

By analyzing and understanding Latin, Greek, and Anglo-Saxon word roots, prefixes, and suffixes, one can better understand word meanings. Of course, people can always look words up in a dictionary or thesaurus, if available, but meaning can often be gleaned on the spot if the reader learns to dissect and examine words.

A word can consist of the following combinations:

- root
- root + suffix
- prefix + root
- prefix + root + suffix

For example, if someone was unfamiliar with the word *submarine,* they could break the word into its parts.

prefix + root

sub + marine

It can be determined that *sub* means *below* as in *subway* and *subpar*. Additionally, one can determine that *marine* refers to *the sea* as in *marine life*. Thus, it can be figured that *submarine* refers to something below the water.

Roots

Roots are the basic components of words. Many roots can stand alone as individual words, but others must be combined with a prefix or suffix to be a word. For example, *calc* is a root but it needs a suffix to be an actual word (*calcium*).

Prefixes

A **prefix** is a word, letter, or number that is placed before another. It adjusts or qualifies the root word's meaning. When written alone, prefixes are followed by a dash to indicate that the root word follows. Some of the most common prefixes are the following:

Prefix	**Meaning**	**Example**
dis-	not or opposite of	disabled
in-, im-, il-, ir-	not	illiterate
re-	again	return
un-	not	unpredictable
anti-	against	antibacterial
fore-	before	forefront
mis-	wrongly	misunderstand
non-	not	nonsense
over-	more than normal	overabundance
pre-	before	preheat
super-	above	superman

Suffixes

A **suffix** is a letter or group of letters added at the end of a word to form another word. The word created from the root and suffix is either a different tense of the same root (*help + ed = helped*) or a new word (*help + ful = helpful*). When written alone, suffixes are preceded by a dash to indicate that the root word comes before. Some of the most common suffixes are the following:

Suffix	**Meaning**	**Example**
-ed	makes a verb past tense	washed
-ing	makes a verb a present participle verb	washing
-ly	to make characteristic of	lovely
-s, -es	to make more than one	chairs, boxes
-able	can be done	deplorable
-al	having characteristics of	comical
-est	comparative	greatest
-ful	full of	wonderful
-ism	belief in	communism
-less	without	faithless
-ment	action or process	accomplishment
-ness	state of	happiness
-ize, -ise	to render, to make	sterilize, advertise
-cede, -ceed, -sede	go	concede, proceed, supersede

Here are some helpful tips:

- When adding a suffix that starts with a vowel (for example, *-ed*) to a one-syllable root whose vowel has a short sound and ends in a consonant (for example, *stun*), the final consonant of the root (*n*) gets doubled.

    stun + ed = stun*n*ed

- Exception: If the past tense verb ends in *x* such as *box*, the *x* does not get doubled.

    box + ed = boxed

- If adding a suffix that starts with a vowel (*-er*) to a multi-syllable word ending in a consonant (*begin*), the consonant (*n*) is doubled.

    begin + er = begin*n*er

- If a short vowel is followed by two or more consonants in a word such as *i+t+c+h = itch,* the last consonant should not be doubled.

    itch + ed = itched

- If adding a suffix that starts with a vowel (*-ing*) to a word ending in *e* (for example, *name*), that word's final *e* is generally (but not always) dropped.

    name + ing = naming
    exception: manage + able = manag*e*able

- If adding a suffix that starts with a consonant (*-ness*) to a word ending in *e* (*complete*), the *e* generally (but not always) remains.

    complete + ness = completeness
    exception: judge + ment = judgment

- There is great diversity on handling words that end in *y*. For words ending in a vowel + *y*, nothing changes in the original word.

    play + ed = played

- For words ending in a consonant + *y*, the *y* is changed to i when adding any suffix except for –*ing*.

    marry + ed = married
    marry + ing = marrying

Evidence and Support

Identifying Relevant Information During Research

Relevant information is that which is pertinent to the topic at hand. Particularly when doing research online, it is easy for students to get overwhelmed with the wealth of information available to them.

Before conducting research, then, students need to begin with a clear idea of the question they want to answer.

For example, a student may be interested in learning more about marriage practices in Jane Austen's England. If that student types "marriage" into a search engine, he or she will have to sift through thousands of unrelated sites before finding anything related to that topic. Narrowing down search parameters can aid in locating relevant information.

When using a book, students can consult the table of contents, glossary, or index to discover whether the book contains relevant information before using it as a resource. If the student finds a hefty volume on Jane Austen, he or she can flip to the index in the back, look for the word *marriage*, and find out how many page references are listed in the book. If there are few or no references to the subject, it is probably not a relevant or useful source.

In evaluating research articles, students may also consult the title, abstract, and keywords before reading the article in its entirety. Referring to the date of publication will also determine whether the research contains up-to-date discoveries, theories, and ideas about the subject, or whether it is outdated.

Evaluating the Credibility of a Print or Digital Source

There are several additional criteria that need to be examined before using a source for a research topic.

The following questions will help determine whether a source is credible:

- Author
  - Who is he or she?
  - Does he or she have the appropriate credentials—e.g., M.D, PhD?
  - Is this person authorized to write on the matter through his/her job or personal experiences?
  - Is he or she affiliated with any known credible individuals or organizations?
  - Has he or she written anything else?
- Publisher
  - Who published/produced the work? Is it a well-known journal, like National Geographic, or a tabloid, like The National Enquirer?
  - Is the publisher from a scholarly, commercial, or government association?
  - Do they publish works related to specific fields?
  - Have they published other works?
  - If a digital source, what kind of website hosts the text? Does it end in .edu, .org, or .com?
- Bias
  - Is the writing objective? Does it contain any loaded or emotional language?
  - Does the publisher/producer have a known bias, such as Fox News or CNN?
  - Does the work include diverse opinions or perspectives?
  - Does the author have any known bias—e.g., Michael Moore, Bill O'Reilly, or the Pope? Is he or she affiliated with any organizations or individuals that may have a known bias—e.g., Citizens United or the National Rifle Association?
  - Does the magazine, book, journal, or website contain any advertising?

- References
    - Are there any references?
    - Are the references credible? Do they follow the same criteria as stated above?
    - Are the references from a related field?
- Accuracy/reliability
    - Has the article, book, or digital source been peer reviewed?
    - Are all of the conclusions, supporting details, or ideas backed with published evidence?
    - If a digital source, is it free of grammatical errors, poor spelling, and improper English?
    - Do other published individuals have similar findings?
- Coverage
    - Are the topic and related material both successfully addressed?
    - Does the work add new information or theories to those of their sources?
    - Is the target audience appropriate for the intended purpose?

Identifying the Appropriate Source for Locating Information

With a wealth of information at people's fingertips in this digital age, it's important to know not only the type of information one is looking for, but also in what medium he or she is most likely to find it. Information needs to be specific and reliable. For example, if someone is repairing a car, an encyclopedia would be mostly useless. While an encyclopedia might include information about cars, an owner's manual will contain the specific information needed for repairs. Information must also be reliable or credible so that it can be trusted. A well-known newspaper may have reliable information, but a peer-reviewed journal article will have likely gone through a more rigorous check for validity. Determining **bias** can be helpful in determining credibility. If the information source (person, organization, or company) has something to gain from the reader forming a certain view on a topic, it's likely the information is skewed. For example, if trying to find the unemployment rate, the Bureau of Labor Statistics is a more credible source than a politician's speech.

Primary sources are best defined as records or items that serve as evidence of periods of history. To be considered primary, the source documents or objects must have been created during the time period in which they reference. Examples include diaries, newspaper articles, speeches, government documents, photographs, and historical artifacts. In today's digital age, primary sources, which were once in print, are often embedded in secondary sources. **Secondary sources**—such as websites, history books, databases, or reviews—contain analysis or commentary on primary sources. Secondary sources borrow information from primary sources through the process of quoting, summarizing, or paraphrasing.

Today's students often complete research online through **electronic sources**. Electronic sources offer advantages over print, and can be accessed on virtually any computer, while libraries or other research centers are limited to fixed locations and specific catalogs. Electronic sources are also efficient and yield massive amounts of data in seconds. The user can tailor a search based on key words, publication years, and article length. Lastly, many **databases** provide the user with instant citations, saving the user the trouble of manually assembling sources for a bibliography.

Although electronic sources yield powerful results, researchers must use caution. While there are many reputable and reliable sources on the internet, just as many are unreliable or biased sources. It's up to the researcher to examine and verify the reliability of sources. *Wikipedia*, for example, may or may not be accurate, depending on the contributor. Many databases, such as *EBSCO* or *SIRS*, offer peer-reviewed articles, meaning the publications have been reviewed for the quality and accuracy of their content.

Identifying Information from a Graphic Representation of Information

Texts may have graphic representations to help illustrate and visually support assertions made. For example, graphics can be used to express samples or segments of a population or demonstrate growth or decay. Three of the most popular graphic formats include line graphs, bar graphs, and pie charts.

Line graphs rely on a horizontal X axis and a vertical Y axis to establish baseline values. Dots are plotted where the horizontal and vertical axes intersect, and those dots are connected with lines. Compared to bar graphs or pie charts, line graphs are more useful for looking at the past and present and predicting future outcomes. For instance, a potential investor would look for stocks that demonstrated steady growth over many decades when examining the stock market. Note that severe spikes up and down indicate instability, while line graphs that display a slow but steady increase may indicate good returns.

Here's an example of a bar graph:

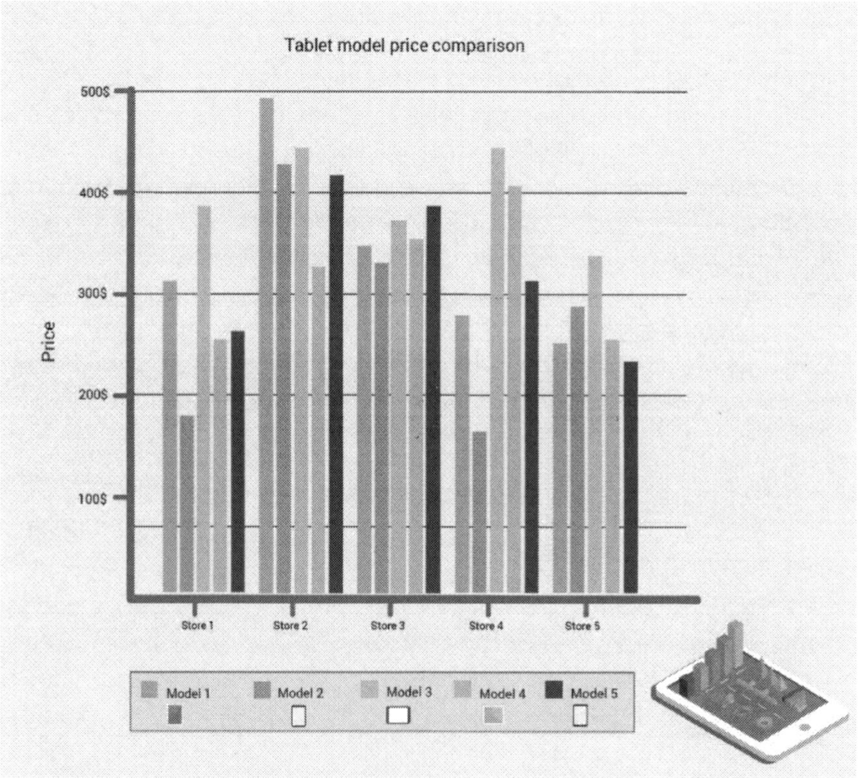

Bar graphs are usually displayed on a vertical Y axis. The bars themselves can be two- or three-dimensional, depending on the designer's tastes. Unlike a line graph, which shows the fluctuation of only one variable, the X axis on a bar graph is excellent for making comparisons, because it shows differences between several variables. For instance, if a consumer wanted to buy a new tablet, she could narrow the selection down to a few choices by using a bar graph to plot the prices side by side. The tallest bar would be the most expensive tablet, the shortest bar would be the cheapest.

A pie chart is divided into wedges that represent a numerical piece of the whole. Pie charts are useful for demonstrating how different categories add up to 100 percent. However, pie charts are not useful in comparing dissimilar items. High schools tend to use pie charts to track where students end up after graduation. Each wedge, for instance, might be labeled *vocational school*, *two-year college*, *four-year college*, *workforce*, or *unemployed*. By calculating the size of each wedge, schools can offer classes in the same ratios as where students will end up after high school. Pie charts are also useful for tracking finances. Items such as car payments, insurance, rent, credit cards, and entertainment would each get their own wedge proportional to the amount spent in a given time period. If one wedge is inordinately bigger than the rest, or if a wedge is expendable, it might be time to create a new financial strategy.

Identifying Scale Readings

Most measuring instruments have scales to allow someone to determine precise measurement. Many of these instruments are becoming digitized, such as their screens' output measurements; for example, weighing scales and tire-pressure gauges often have digital screens. However, it's still important to know how to read scales. Many rulers have scales for inches on one side and scales for centimeters on the other side. On the inches' side, the longest black lines indicate the inch marks, and the slightly shorter lines indicate the half-inch marks. Progressively shorter black lines indicate the quarter-inch, eighth-inch, and sometimes even sixteenth-inch marks.

Using Legends and Map Keys

Legends and map keys are placed on maps to identify what the symbols on the map represent. Generally, map symbols stand for things like railroads, national or state highways, and public parks. Legends and maps keys can generally be found in the bottom right corner of a map. They are necessary to avoid the needless repetition of the same information because of the large amounts of information condensed onto a map. In addition, there may be a compass rose that shows the directions of north, south, east, and west. Most maps are oriented such that the top of the map is north.

Maps also have scales, which are a type of legend or key that show relative distances between fixed points. If you were on a highway and nearly out of gas, a map's scale would help you determine if you could make it to the next town before running out of fuel.

Making Inferences

There are a few ways for readers to engage actively with the text, such as making inferences and predictions. An **inference** refers to a point that is implied (as opposed to directly-stated) by the evidence presented:

> Bradley packed up all of the items from his desk in a box and said goodbye to his coworkers for the last time.

From this sentence, though it is not directly stated, readers can infer that Bradley is leaving his job. It's necessary to use inference in order to draw conclusions about the meaning of a passage. Authors make implications through character dialogue, thoughts, effects on others, actions, and looks. Like in life, readers must assemble all the clues to form a complete picture.

When making an inference about a passage, it's important to rely only on the information that is provided in the text itself. This helps readers ensure that their conclusions are valid.

Readers will also find themselves making predictions when reading a passage or paragraph. *Predictions* are guesses about what's going to happen next. Readers can use prior knowledge to help make accurate predictions. Prior knowledge is best utilized when readers make links between the current text, previously read texts, and life experiences. Some texts use suspense and foreshadowing to captivate readers:

A cat darted across the street just as the car came careening around the curve.

One unfortunate prediction might be that the car will hit the cat. Of course, predictions aren't always accurate, so it's important to read carefully to the end of the text to determine the accuracy of predictions.

Information that is Explicitly Stated

As a reader, you will want to draw a conclusion about what the author has presented. **Drawing a conclusion** will help you to understand what the writer intended as well as whether you agree with what he or she has said. There are a few ways to determine the logical conclusion, but careful reading is the most important. Read the passage a few times and highlight or take notes on the details that you deem important to the meaning of the piece. You may draw a conclusion that is different than what the writer intended, or you may draw more than one conclusion. Look carefully at the details to see if your conclusion matches up with what the writer has presented and intended for readers to understand. Of course, in the test itself, you may not have time to take notes or compare. However, it may be helpful to practice this on your own to make sure your comprehension skills are strong.

Textual evidence can help readers to draw a conclusion about a passage. Textual evidence refers to information such as facts and examples that support the main point. Textual evidence will likely come from outside sources and can be in the form of quoted or paraphrased material. Look to this evidence and its credibility and validity in relation to the main idea to draw a conclusion about the writing.

Consider that the author may state the conclusion directly in the passage. Inferring the author's conclusion is useful, especially when it is not overtly stated, but inferences should not outweigh the information that is directly stated. Alternatively, when readers are trying to draw a conclusion about a text, it may not always be directly stated.

As mentioned, a summary is another effective way to draw a conclusion from a passage. A **summary** is a shortened version of the original text, written in one's own words. It should focus on the main points of the original text, including only the relevant details. It's important to be brief but thorough in a summary. While the summary should always be shorter than the original passage, it should still retain the meaning of the original source.

Like summarizing, paraphrasing can also help a reader to fully understand a part of a reading. **Paraphrasing** requires the reader to take a small part of the passage and to say it in their own words. Paraphrasing is more than rewording the original passage, though. It should be written in one's own way, while still retaining the meaning of the original source. When a reader's goal is to write something in their own words, deeper understanding of the original source is required. Again, working to summarize or paraphrase each passage on the test may not be the most efficient use of your time. However, think about these tools when practicing comprehending passages. Once you are familiar with carefully selecting important aspects of the passage, it will come easier to you on test day.

Use of Reference Materials

Reference materials are indispensable tools for beginners and experts alike. Becoming a competent English communicator doesn't necessarily mean memorizing every single rule about spelling, grammar, or punctuation—it means knowing where and how to find accurate information about the rules of English usage. Students of English have a wide variety of references materials available to them, and, in an increasingly digitized world, more and more of these materials can be found online or as easily-accessible phone applications. Educators should introduce students to different types of reference materials as well as when and how to use them.

Spell Check

Most word processing software programs come equipped with a spell-checking feature. Web browsers and personal devices like smartphones and tablets may also have a spell checker enabled. *Spell check* automatically detects misspelled words and suggests alternate spellings. Many writers have come to rely on spell check due to its convenience and ease of use. However, there are some caveats to using spell check—it only checks whether a word is spelled correctly, not if it is used correctly. As discussed above, there are numerous examples of commonly-confused words in English, the misuse of which may not be detected by a spell checker. Many word processing programs do integrate spell checking and grammar checking functions, however. Thus, although running a spell check is an important part of reviewing any piece of writing, it should not be the only step of the review process. Further, spell checkers recommend correctly-spelled words based on an approximation of the misspelled word, so writers need to be somewhat close to the correct spelling in order for spell check to be useful.

Dictionary

Dictionaries are readily available in print, digital formats, and as mobile apps. A dictionary offers a wealth of information to users. First, in the absence of spell-checking software, a *dictionary* can be used to identify correct spelling and to determine the word's pronunciation—often written using the International Phonetic Alphabet (IPA). Perhaps the best-known feature of a dictionary is its explanation of a word's meanings, as a single word can have multiple definitions. A dictionary organizes these definitions based on their parts of speech and then arranges them from most to least commonly used meanings or from oldest to most modern usage. Many dictionaries also offer information about a word's etymology and usage. With all these functions, then, a dictionary is a basic, essential tool in many situations. Students can turn to a dictionary when they encounter an unfamiliar word or when they see a familiar word used in a new way.

There are many dictionaries to choose from, but perhaps the most highly respected source is the *Oxford English Dictionary* (OED). The OED is a historical dictionary, and as such, all entries include quotes of the word as it has been used throughout history. Users of the OED can get a deeper sense of a word's evolution over time and in different parts of the world. Another standard dictionary in America is *Merriam-Webster*.

Thesaurus

Whereas a dictionary entry lists a word's definitions, a *thesaurus* entry lists a word's *synonyms* and *antonyms*—i.e., words with similar and opposite meanings, respectively. A dictionary can be used to find out what a word means and where it came from, and a thesaurus can be used to understand a word's relationship to other words. A thesaurus can be a powerful vocabulary-building tool. By becoming familiar with synonyms and antonyms, students will be more equipped to use a broad range of vocabulary in their speech and writing. Of course, one thing to be aware of when using a thesaurus is that most words do not have exact synonyms. Rather, there are slight nuances of meaning that can make one word more appropriate than another in a given context. In this case, it is often to the user's advantage to consult a thesaurus side-by-side with a dictionary to confirm any differences in usage between two synonyms. Some digital sources, such as *Dictionary.com*, integrate a dictionary and a thesaurus.

Generally, though, a thesaurus is a useful tool to help writers add variety and precision to their word choice. Consulting a thesaurus can help students elevate their writing to an appropriate academic level by replacing vague or overused words with more expressive or academic ones. Also, word processors often offer a built-in thesaurus, making it easy for writers to look up synonyms and vary word choice as they work.

Glossary
A *glossary* is similar to a dictionary in that it offers an explanation of terms. However, while a dictionary attempts to cover every word in a language, a glossary only focuses on those terms relevant to a specific field. Also, a glossary entry is more likely to offer a longer explanation of a term and its relevance within that field. Glossaries are often found at the back of textbooks or other nonfiction publications in order to explain new or unfamiliar terms to readers. A glossary may also be an entire book on its own that covers all of the essential terms and concepts within a particular profession, field, or other specialized area of knowledge. For learners seeking general definitions of terms from any context, then, a dictionary is an appropriate reference source, but for students of specialized fields, a glossary will usually provide more in-depth information.

Style Manual
Many rules of English usage are standard, but other rules may be more subjective. An example can be seen in the following structures:

A. I went to the store and bought eggs, milk, and bread.
B. I went to the store and bought eggs, milk and bread.

The final comma in a list before *and* or *or* is known as an Oxford comma or serial comma. It is, recommended in some styles, but not in others. To determine the appropriate use of the Oxford comma, writers can consult a style manual.

A *style manual* is a comprehensive collection of guidelines for language use and document formatting. Some fields refer to a common style guide—e.g., the Associated Press or *AP Stylebook*, a standard in American journalism. Individual organizations may rely on their own house style. Regardless, the purpose of a style manual is to ensure uniformity across all documents. Style manuals explain things such as how to format titles, when to write out numbers or use numerals, and how to cite sources. Because there are many different style guides, students should know how and when to consult an appropriate guide. The Chicago Manual of Style is common in the publication of books and academic journals. The Modern Language Association style (MLA) is another commonly used academic style format, while the American Psychological Association style (APA) may be used for scientific publications. Familiarity with using a style guide is particularly important for students who are college bound or pursuing careers in academic or professional writing.

In the examples above, the Oxford comma is recommended by the Chicago Manual of Style, so sentence A would be correct if the writer is using this style. But the comma is not recommended by the *AP Stylebook*, so sentence B would be correct if the writer is using the AP style.

General Grammar and Style References
Any language arts textbook should offer general grammatical and stylistic advice to students, but there are a few well-respected texts that can also be used for reference. *Elements of Style* by William Strunk is regularly assigned to students as a guide on effective written communication, including how to avoid common usage mistakes and how to make the most of parallel structure. *Garner's Modern American Usage* by Bryan Garner is another text that guides students on how to achieve precision and understandability in their writing. Whereas other reference sources discussed above tend to address specific language concerns, these types of texts offer a more holistic approach to cultivating effective language skills.

Electronic Resources

With print texts, it is easy to identify the authors and their credentials, as well as the publisher and their reputation. With electronic resources like websites, though, it can be trickier to assess the reliability of information. Students should be alert when gathering information from the Internet. Understanding the significance of website *domains*—which include identification strings of a site—can help. Website domains ending in *.edu* are educational sites and tend to offer more reliable research in their field. A *.org* ending tends to be used by nonprofit organizations and other community groups, *.com* indicates a privately-owned website, and a *.gov* site is run by the government. Websites affiliated with official organizations, research groups, or institutes of learning are more likely to offer relevant, fact-checked, and reliable information.

Integration of Resource Material

It can be daunting to integrate so many sources into a research paper while st*ill maintaining fluency and coherency. Most source material is incorporated in the form of quotations or paraphrases, while citing the source at the end of their respective references.*

There are several guidelines to consider when integrating a source into writing:

- The piece should be written in the author's voice. Quotations, especially long ones, should be limited and spaced evenly throughout the paper.

- All paragraphs should begin with the author's own words and end with his or her own words; quotations should never start or end a paragraph.

- Quotations and paraphrases should be used to emphasize a point, give weight to an idea, and validate a claim.

- Supporting evidence should be introduced in a sentence or paragraph, and then explained afterwards: According to Waters (1979) [signal phrase], "All in all, we're just another brick in the wall" (p.24). The wall suggests that people are becoming more alienated, and the bricks symbolize a paradoxical connection to that alienation [Explanation].

- When introducing a source for the first time, the author's name and a smooth transition should be included: In Pink Floyd's groundbreaking album The Wall, Roger Waters argues that society is causing people to become more alienated.

- There should be an even balance between quotations and paraphrases.

- Quotations or paraphrases should never be taken out of context in a way that alters the original author's intent.

- Quotations should be syntactically and grammatically integrated.

- Quotations should not simply be copied and pasted in the paper, rather, they should be introduced into a paper with natural transitions.

o As argued in Johnson's article…
o Evidence of this point can be found in Johnson's article, where she asserts that…
o The central argument of John's article is…

Documentation of Sources

Identifying the Components of a Citation
Citation styles vary according to which style guide is consulted. Examples of commonly-used styles include MLA, APA, and Chicago/Turabian. Each citation style includes similar components, although the order and formatting of these components varies.

MLA Style
For an MLA style citation, components must be included or excluded depending on the source, so writers should determine which components are applicable to the source being cited. Here are the basic components:

- Author—last name, first name
- Title of source
- Title of container—e.g., a journal title or website
- Other contributors—e.g., editor or translator
- Version
- Number
- Publisher
- Publication date
- Location—e.g., the URL or DOI
- Date of Access—optional

APA Style
The following components can be found in APA style citations. Components must be included or excluded depending on the source, so writers should determine which components are applicable to the source being cited.

The basic components are as follows:

- Author—last name, first initial, middle initial
- Publication date
- Title of chapter, article, or text
- Editor—last name, first initial, middle initial
- Version/volume
- Number/issue
- Page numbers
- DOI or URL
- Database—if article is difficult to locate
- City of publication
- State of publication, abbreviated
- Publisher

Chicago/Turabian Style
Chicago/Turabian style citations are also referred to as note systems and are used most frequently in the humanities and the arts. Components must be included or excluded depending on the source, so

writers should determine which components are applicable to the source being cited. They contain the following elements:

- Author—last name, first name, middle initial
- Title of chapter or article—in quotation marks
- Title of source
- Editor—first name, last name
- Page numbers
- Version/volume
- Number/issue
- Page numbers
- Date of access
- DOI
- Publication location—city and state abbreviation/country
- Publisher
- Publication Date

Citing Source Material Appropriately
The following information contains examples of the common types of sources used in research as well as the formats for each citation style. First lines of citation entries are presented flush to the left margin, and second/subsequent details are presented with a hanging indent. Some examples of bibliography entries are presented below:

Book

- MLA
  Format: Last name, First name, Middle initial. *Title of Source*. Publisher, Publication Date.
  Example: Sampson, Maximus R. *Diaries from an Alien Invasion*. Campbell Press, 1989.
- APA
  Format: Last name, First initial, Middle initial. (Year Published) *Book Title.* City, State: Publisher.
  Example: Sampson, M. R. (1989). *Diaries from an Alien Invasion. Springfield, IL*: Campbell Press.
- Chicago/Turabian
  Format: Last name, First name, Middle initial. *Book Title*. City, State: Publisher, Year of publication.
  Example: Sampson, Maximus R. *Diaries from an Alien Invasion. Springfield, IL*: Campbell Press, 1989.

A Chapter in an Edited Book

- MLA
  Format: Last name, First name, Middle initial. "Title of Source." *Title of Container*, Other Contributors, Publisher, Publication Date, Location.
  Example: Sampson, Maximus R. "The Spaceship." *Diaries from an Alien Invasion*, edited by Allegra M. Brewer, Campbell Press, 1989, pp. 45-62.
- APA
  Format: Last name, First Initial, Middle initial. (Year Published) Chapter title. In First initial, Middle initial, Last Name (Ed.), *Book title* (pp. page numbers). City, State: Publisher.
  Example: Sampson, M. R. (1989). The Spaceship. In A. M. Brewer (Ed.), *Diaries from an Alien Invasion* (pp. 45-62). Springfield, IL: Campbell Press.

- Chicago/Turabian
  Format: Last name, First name, Middle initial. "Chapter Title." In Book Title, edited by Editor's Name (First, Middle In. Last), Page(s). City: Publisher, Year Published.
  Example: Sampson, Maximus R. "The Spaceship," in *Diaries from an Alien Invasion*, edited by Allegra M. Brewer, 45-62. Springfield: Campbell Press, 1989.

Article in a Journal

- MLA
  Format: Last name, First name, Middle initial. "Title of Source." *Title of Journal*, Number, Publication Date, Location.
  Example: Rowe, Jason R. "The Grief Monster." *Strong Living*, vol. 9, no. 9, 2016, pp 25-31.
- APA
  Format: Last name, First initial, Middle initial. (Year Published). Title of article. *Name of Journal, volume*(issue), page(s).
  Example: Rowe, J. R. (2016). The grief monster. *Strong Living, 9*(9), 25-31.
- Chicago/Turabian:
  Format: Last name, First name, Middle initial. "Title of Article." *Name of Journal* volume, issue (Year Published): Page(s).
  Example: Rowe, Jason, R. "The Grief Monster." *Strong Living* 9, no. 9 (2016): 25-31.

Page on a Website

- MLA
  Format: Last name, First name, Middle initial. "Title of Article." *Name of Website*, date published (Day Month Year), URL. Date accessed (Day Month Year).
  Example: Rowe, Jason. "The Grief Monster." *Strong Living Online*, 9 Sept. 2016. http://www.somanylosses.com/the-grief-monster/html. Accessed 13 Sept. 2016.
- APA
  Format: Last name, First initial. Middle initial. (Date Published—Year, Month Day). Page or article title. Retrieved from URL
  Example: Rowe, J. W. (2016, Sept. 9). The grief monster. Retrieved from http://www.somanylosses.com/ the-grief-monster/html
- Chicago/Turabian
  Format: Last Name, First Name, Middle initial. "Page Title." *Website Title*. Last modified Month day, year. Accessed month, day, year. URL.
  Example: Rowe, Jason. "The Grief Monster." Strong Living Online. Last modified September 9, 2016. Accessed September 13, 2016. http://www.somanylosses.com/the-grief-monster/html.

In-Text Citations

Most of the content found in a research paper will be supporting evidence that must be cited in-text, i.e., directly after the sentence that makes the statement. In-text citations contain details that correspond to the first detail in the bibliography entry—usually the author.

- MLA style - In-text citations will contain the author and the page number (if the source has page numbers) for direct quotations. Paraphrased source material may have just the author.
  - According to Johnson, liver cancer treatment is "just beyond our reach" (976).
  - The treatment of liver cancer is not within our reach, currently (Johnson).
  - The narrator opens the story with a paradoxical description: "It was the best of times, it was the worst of times" (Dickens 1).

- APA Style - In text citations will contain the author, the year of publication, and a page marker—if the source is paginated—for direct quotations. Paraphrased source material will include the author and year of publication.
    - According to Johnson (1986), liver cancer treatment is "just beyond our reach" (p. 976).
    - The treatment of liver cancer is not within our reach, currently (Johnson, 1986).

- Chicago Style - Chicago style has two approaches to in-text citation: notes and bibliography or author-date.
    - Notes – There are two options for notes: endnotes—provided in a sequential list at the end of the paper and separate from bibliography—or footnotes provided at the bottom of a page. In either case, the use of superscript indicates the citation number.
        - Johnson states that treatment of liver cancer is "just beyond our reach." [1]
        - 1. Robert W. Johnson, Oncology in the Twenty-first Century (Kentville, Nova Scotia: Kentville Publishing, 1986), 159.

- Author-Date – The author-date system includes the author's name, publication year, and page number.
    - Johnson states that treatment of liver cancer is "just beyond our reach" (1986, 159).

Practice Questions

In this excerpt from a text set in nineteenth-century France, two friends, Albert de Morcerf and the Count of Monte Cristo, discuss Parisian social life. Read it and answer questions 1–12.

"Mademoiselle Eugénie is pretty—I think I remember that to be her name."

"Very pretty, or rather, very beautiful," replied Albert, "but of that style of beauty which I don't appreciate; I am an ungrateful fellow."

"Really," said Monte Cristo, lowering his voice, "you don't appear to me to be very enthusiastic on the subject of this marriage."

"Mademoiselle Danglars is too rich for me," replied Morcerf, "and that frightens me."

"Bah," exclaimed Monte Cristo, "that's a fine reason to give. Are you not rich yourself?"

"My father's income is about 50,000 francs per annum; and he will give me, perhaps, ten or twelve thousand when I marry."

"That, perhaps, might not be considered a large sum, in Paris especially," said the count; "but everything doesn't depend on wealth, and it's a fine thing to have a good name, and to occupy a high station in society. Your name is celebrated, your position magnificent; and then the Comte de Morcerf is a soldier, and it's pleasing to see the integrity of a Bayard united to the poverty of a Duguesclin; disinterestedness is the brightest ray in which a noble sword can shine. As for me, I consider the union with Mademoiselle Danglars a most suitable one; she will enrich you, and you will ennoble her."

Albert shook his head and looked thoughtful. "There is still something else," said he.

"I confess," observed Monte Cristo, "that I have some difficulty in comprehending your objection to a young lady who is both rich and beautiful."

"Oh," said Morcerf, "this repugnance, if repugnance it may be called, isn't all on my side."

"Whence can it arise, then? for you told me your father desired the marriage."

"It's my mother who dissents; she has a clear and penetrating judgment and doesn't smile on the proposed union. I cannot account for it, but she seems to entertain some prejudice against the Danglars."

"Ah," said the count, in a somewhat forced tone, "that may be easily explained; the Comtesse de Morcerf, who is aristocracy and refinement itself, doesn't relish the idea of being allied by your marriage with one of ignoble birth; that is natural enough."

1. The meaning of the word "repugnance" is closest to:
   a. Strong resemblance
   b. Strong dislike
   c. Extreme shyness
   d. Extreme dissimilarity
   e. Intense suffering

2. What can be inferred about Albert's family?
   a. Their finances are uncertain.
   b. Albert is the only son in his family.
   c. Their name is more respected than the Danglars'.
   d. Albert's mother and father both agree on their decisions.
   e. No one wants Albert to be married at all.

3. What is Albert's attitude towards his impending marriage?
   a. Pragmatic
   b. Romantic
   c. Indifferent
   d. Apprehensive
   e. Animosity

4. What is the best description of the Count's relationship with Albert?
   a. He's like a strict parent, criticizing Albert's choices.
   b. He's like a wise uncle, giving practical advice to Albert.
   c. He's like a close friend, supporting all of Albert's opinions.
   d. He's like a suspicious investigator, asking many probing questions.
   e. He's like a stranger, listening politely but offering no advice.

5. Which sentence is true of Albert's mother?
   a. She belongs to a noble family.
   b. She often makes poor choices.
   c. She is primarily occupied with money.
   d. She is unconcerned about her son's future.
   e. She is supportive of the upcoming marriage.

6. Based on this passage, what is probably NOT true about French society in the 1800s?
   a. Children often received money from their parents.
   b. Marriages were sometimes arranged between families.
   c. Marriages were expected to be economically or socially beneficial to family.
   d. People were often expected to marry within their same social class.
   e. The richest people in society were also the most respected.

7. Why is the Count puzzled by Albert's attitude toward his marriage?
   a. He seems reluctant to marry Eugénie, despite her wealth and beauty.
   b. He is marrying against his father's wishes, despite usually following his advice.
   c. He appears excited to marry someone he doesn't love, despite being a hopeless romantic.
   d. He expresses reverence towards Eugénie, despite being from a higher social class than her.
   e. Albert knows the Count loved Eugénie first, yet he is still marrying her.

8. The passage is made up mostly of what kind of text?
   a. Narration
   b. Dialogue
   c. Description
   d. Explanation
   e. Information

9. What does the word "ennoble" mean in the middle of the passage?
    a. to create beauty in another person
    b. to endow someone with wealth
    c. to make someone chaste again
    d. to give someone a noble rank or title
    e. to provide someone with great joy

10. Why is the count said to have a "forced tone" in the last paragraph?
    a. Because he is in love with Mademoiselle Eugénie and is trying to keep it a secret.
    b. Because he finally agrees with Albert's point of view but still doesn't understand it.
    c. Because he finally understands Albert's point of view but still doesn't agree with it.
    d. Because he is only pretending that Albert is his friend to get information out of him.
    e. Because he is annoyed that Albert is getting married instead of himself.

11. Which of the following is true about Albert's father?
    a. He is a thief.
    b. He is a peasant.
    c. He is a king.
    d. He is a gangster.
    e. He is a soldier.

12. Which of the following types of literature does this text most likely belong to?
    a. Biography
    b. Drama
    c. Epic poem
    d. Autobiography
    e. Fiction novel

Questions 13–24 are based upon the following passage:

> "MANKIND being originally equals in the order of creation, the equality could only be destroyed by some subsequent circumstance; the distinctions of rich, and poor, may in a great measure be accounted for, and that without having recourse to the harsh ill sounding names of oppression and avarice. Oppression is often the consequence, but seldom or never the means of riches; and though avarice will preserve a man from being necessitously poor, it generally makes him too timorous to be wealthy.
>
> But there is another and greater distinction for which no truly natural or religious reason can be assigned, and that is, the distinction of men into KINGS and SUBJECTS. Male and female are the distinctions of nature, good and bad the distinctions of heaven; but how a race of men came into the world so exalted above the rest, and distinguished like some new species, is worth enquiring into, and whether they are the means of happiness or of misery to mankind.
>
> In the early ages of the world, according to the scripture chronology, there were no kings; the consequence of which was there were no wars; it is the pride of kings which throw mankind into confusion. Holland without a king hath enjoyed more peace for this last century than any of the monarchical governments in Europe. Antiquity favors the same remark; for the quiet and rural lives of the first patriarchs hath a happy something in them, which vanishes away when we come to the history of Jewish royalty.

Government by kings was first introduced into the world by the Heathens, from whom the children of Israel copied the custom. It was the most prosperous invention the Devil ever set on foot for the promotion of idolatry. The Heathens paid divine honors to their deceased kings, and the Christian world hath improved on the plan by doing the same to their living ones. How impious is the title of sacred majesty applied to a worm, who in the midst of his splendor is crumbling into dust!

As the exalting one man so greatly above the rest cannot be justified on the equal rights of nature, so neither can it be defended on the authority of scripture; for the will of the Almighty, as declared by Gideon and the prophet Samuel, expressly disapproves of government by kings. All anti-monarchical parts of scripture have been very smoothly glossed over in monarchical governments, but they undoubtedly merit the attention of countries, which have their governments yet to form. "Render unto Caesar the things which are Caesar's" is the scripture doctrine of courts, yet it is no support of monarchical government, for the Jews at that time were without a king, and in a state of vassalage to the Romans.

Near three thousand years passed away from the Mosaic account of the creation, till the Jews under a national delusion requested a king. Till then their form of government (except in extraordinary cases, where the Almighty interposed) was a kind of republic administered by a judge and the elders of the tribes. Kings they had none, and it was held sinful to acknowledge any being under that title but the Lord of Hosts. And when a man seriously reflects on the idolatrous homage which is paid to the persons of Kings, he need not wonder, that the Almighty ever jealous of his honor, should disapprove of a form of government which so impiously invades the prerogative of heaven.

Excerpt From: Thomas Paine. "Common Sense."

13. According to passage, what role does avarice, or greed, play in poverty?
    a. It can make a man very wealthy..
    b. It is the consequence of wealth..
    c. Avarice can prevent a man from being poor, but too fearful to be very wealthy..
    d. Avarice is what drives a person to be very poor..
    e. Avarice is seen by impoverished people as a great evil..

14. Of these distinctions, which does the author believe to be beyond natural or religious reason?
    a. Good and bad
    b. Male and female
    c. Human and animal
    d. King and subjects
    e. Faith and fear

15. According to the passage, what are the Heathens responsible for?
    a. Government by kings
    b. Quiet and rural lives of patriarchs
    c. Paying divine honors to their living kings
    d. Equal rights of nature
    e. The Mosaic account of creation

16. Which of the following best states Paine's rationale for the denouncement of monarchy?
    a. It is against the laws of nature..
    b. It is against the equal rights of nature and is denounced in scripture..
    c. Despite scripture, a monarchal government is unlawful..
    d. Neither the law nor scripture denounce monarchy..
    e. It has been denounced by the Catholic church..

17. Based on the passage, what is the best definition of the word *idolatrous*?
    a. Worshipping heroes
    b. Being deceitful
    c. Sinfulness
    d. Engaging in illegal activities
    e. Being unfaithful to one's partner

18. What is the essential meaning of lines 41-44?

    And when a man seriously reflects on the idolatrous homage which is paid to the persons of Kings, he need not wonder, that the Almighty ever jealous of his honor, should disapprove of a form of government which so impiously invades the prerogative of heaven.

    a. God would disapprove of the irreverence of a monarchical government.
    b. With careful reflection, men should realize that heaven is not promised.
    c. God will punish those that follow a monarchical government.
    d. Belief in a monarchical government cannot coexist with belief in God.
    e. Very few kings have ever believed in or worshipped God.

19. Based on the passage, what is the best definition of the word *timorous* in the first paragraph?
    a. being full of fear
    b. a characteristic of shyness
    c. being able to see through someone
    d. being full of anger and hatred
    e. a characteristic of boldness

20. The author's attitude toward the subject can best be described as:
    a. indifferent and fatigued
    b. impassioned and critical
    c. awed and enchanted
    d. enraged and sulky
    e. contented and upbeat

21. The main purpose of the fourth paragraph is:
    a. To persuade the audience that heathens were more advanced than Christians.
    b. To explain how monarchs came into existence and how Christians adopted the same system.
    c. To describe the divination of English monarchs and how it is their birthright to be revered.
    d. To counteract the preceding paragraph by giving proof of the damage monarchs can cause.
    e. To show how civilizations as a whole are happier and more peaceful without monarchs.

22. In the last paragraph, what does the author mean by the "Mosaic account of creation"?
   a. The author means that creation is based on individuals composed of cells of two genetically different types.
   b. The author implies that the work of God is like a mosaic painting due to the various formations of creation.
   c. The author means that the kings of the past developed a system in which to maintain accounts of creation.
   d. The author implies that the recorded history of creation is a collection, collage, or pattern taken from various accounts of cultures.
   e. The author means that the account of creation that exists is meant to bring comfort to people as a patchwork quilt would comfort someone who is cold.

23. Which of the following types of nonfiction literature does this text most likely belong to?
   a. Diary
   b. Biography
   c. Autobiography
   d. Speech
   e. Essay

24. Which of the following best represents the author's intended audience?
   a. Civilians who are oppressed and are in need of support.
   b. Children who are interested in going to a boarding school.
   c. Subjects of a country who are part of a revolution.
   d. Individuals who are on the fence about the best way to govern a country.
   e. Soldiers who are ready to go to war for their country.

Questions 25–37 are based on the following passages taken from Bradford's History of 'Plimouth Plantation' *by William Bradford, written between 1630 and 1651:*

2. Chap.

Of their departure into Holland and their troubls ther aboute, with some of the many difficulties they found and mete withall.

An^{o}. 1608.

Being thus constrained to leave their native soyle and countrie, their lands & livings, and all their freinds & famillier acquaintance, it was much, and thought marvelous by many. But to goe into a countrie they knew not (but by hearsay), wher they must [16]learne a new language, and get their livings they knew not how, it being a dear place, & subjecte to ye misseries of warr, it was by many thought an adventure almost desperate, a case intolerable, & a misserie worse than death. Yet [8] this was not all, for though they could not stay, yet were ye not suffered to goe, but ye ports and havens were shut against them, so as they were faine to seeke secrete means of conveance, & to bribe & fee ye mariners, & give exterordinarie rates for their passages.

Ther was a large companie of them purposed to get passage at Boston in Lincoln-shire, and for that end had hired a shipe wholy to them selves, & made agreement with the maister to be ready at a certaine day, and take them and their goods in, at a conveniente place, wher they accordingly would all attende [17]in readines. So after long waiting, & large expences, though he kepte not day with them, yet he came at length & tooke them in, in ye night. But when he had them & their goods abord, he betrayed them, haveing before hand complotted with ye serchers & other officers so to doe; who tooke them, and put them into open boats, & ther rifled & ransaked them, searching them to their shirts for money, yea even ye women furder then became modestie; and then caried them back into ye towne, & made them a spectackle & wonder to the multitude, which came flocking on all sids to behould them. Being thus first, by the chatch-poule officers, rifled, & stripte of their money, books, and much other goods, they were presented to ye magestrates, and messengers sente to informe ye lords of ye Counsell of them; and so they were com̃ited to ward. Indeed ye magestrats used them courteously, and shewed them what favour they could; but could not deliver them, till order came from ye Counsell-table. But ye issue was that after a months imprisonmente, ye greatest parte were dismiste, & sent to y^eplaces from whence they came; but 7. of ye principall were still kept in prison, and bound over to ye Assises.

The nexte spring after, ther was another attempte made by some of these & others, to get over at an other place. And it so fell out, that they light of a Dutchman at Hull, having a ship of his owne belonging [18]to Zealand; they made agreemente with him, and acquainted [9] him with their condition, hoping to find more faithfullnes in him, then in ye former of their owne nation. He bad them not fear, for he would doe well enough. He was by appointment to take them in betweene Grimsbe & Hull, wher was a large com̃one a good way distante from any towne. Now aganst the prefixed time, the women & children, with ye goods, were sent to ye place in a small barke, which they had hired for y^t end; and ye men were to meete them by land. But it so fell out, that they were ther a day before ye shipe came, & ye sea being rough, and ye women very sicke, prevailed with ye seamen to put into a creeke hardby, wher they lay on ground at lowwater. The nexte morning ye shipe came, but they were fast, & could not stir till aboute noone. In ye mean time, ye shipe maister, perceiveing how ye matter was, sente his boate to be getting ye men abord whom he saw ready, walking aboute ye shore. But after ye first boat full was gott abord, & she was ready to goe for more, the m^r espied a greate company, both horse & foote, with bills, & gunes, & other weapons; for ye countrie was raised to take them. Y^e Dutch-man seeing y^t, swore his countries oath, "sacremente," and having ye wind faire, waiged his Ancor, hoysed sayles, & away. But y^epoore men which were gott abord, were in great distress for their wives and children, which they saw thus to be [19] taken, and were left destitute of their helps; and them selves also, not having a cloath to shifte them with, more then they had on their baks, & some scarce a peney aboute them, all they had being abord ye barke. It drew tears from their eyes, and any thing they had they would have given to have been a shore againe; but all in vaine, ther was no remedy, they must thus sadly part.

25. Which of the following was NOT a difficulty faced by the group of travelers?
    a. They didn't know the new country's language.
    b. They weren't allowed to bring their wives or children to the new country.
    c. They didn't know how to make a living in the new country.
    d. Ships charged exorbitant rates for the voyage to the new country.
    e. They were met with hostility and prejudice by others in their travels.

26. The Dutchman's "sacramente" was:
    a. a prayer.
    b. an oath.
    c. a ritual.
    d. a promise.
    e. a decree.

27. What went wrong with the ship hired at Boston in Lincoln-shire?
    a. The women got sick due to the rough seas.
    b. The men were separated from their wives and children.
    c. The group couldn't get out of jail in time to board the ship.
    d. The shipmaster betrayed them.
    e. The ship got caught in a storm which caused a shipwreck.

28. Based on the passage, why did the men leave their wives and children?
    a. Armed government officials arrived on the shore.
    b. The government refused to let them out of prison.
    c. The sea was too rough to risk going back for them.
    d. The women were too sick to make the voyage.
    e. The women and children had contracted a disease.

29. Ships charged the group of travelers extra fees because:
    a. they were a vulnerable minority group.
    b. the voyage was particularly long and dangerous.
    c. the government outlawed their departure.
    d. they were wealthy enough to afford it.
    e. the group was so large and rowdy.

30. Based on the passage, which of the following statements BEST describes how the government treated the group of travelers?
    a. The government expelled them from their homeland.
    b. The government persecuted the group due to their different religious beliefs.
    c. The government valued the women and children more than the men.
    d. The government repeatedly tried to stop them from leaving.
    e. The government starved them and kept them from owning property.

31. Which of the following events occurred first?
    a. Some of the group's members were kept in prison and sent to the Assises.
    b. The group became shipwrecked on the shore.
    c. The men cried after getting separated from their wives and children.
    d. The women became sick due to the rough seas.
    e. Government officials embarrassed the group by parading them through town.

32. Which of the following statements best summarizes the second paragraph?
    a. The shipmaster's betrayal led to incredible hardship for the group, including public embarrassment and imprisonment.
    b. The group was imprisoned, and they received better treatment from the magistrates than the lords of the counsel.
    c. The women's sickness led to the government officials discovering, seizing, and imprisoning the group.
    d. While some of the group members were released, others were kept in prison and sent to the Assises.
    e. The women and children make it safely out of town and are met by their husbands shortly afterward.

33. Which of the following statements can reasonably be inferred from the men's reaction at the end of the passage?

a. The men would have to pay even more exorbitant fees and bribes to bring their wives and children to the commune.

b. The men were more upset by the loss of their possessions than the separation from their wives and children.

c. The Dutch shipmaster betrayed them by sailing away instead of attempting to rescue the women and children.

d. There was a strong likelihood that the men wouldn't see their wives and children for a long time.

e. The men were overjoyed at having left, even if it meant they were without their wives or children.

34. How did the wives and children become separated from the men?

a. They were still in prison when the ship set sail.

b They got sick, forcing their boat to take a detour, and they didn't board the ship in time.

c. They were on a separate boat, and the captain of their boat betrayed them.

d. They were pulled off course by strong winds, so they didn't reach the agreed upon meeting place in time.

e. The wives intentionally left the men so that they could escape with just their children.

35. Which of the following describes why the text is full of confusing grammar/language?

a. The author is uneducated and does not know how to write very well.

b. The text was translated from another language and is a poor rendition of the original.

c. The text is from the 1600s and displays how the English language has changed over time.

d. The author wrote it while he was a child, so he was not yet a professional writer.

e. The author wrote it anonymously and changed the spelling and dialect so no one would find out who he was.

36. What type of passage is this?

a. Historical memoir or journal

b. Passage from a textbook

c. Poem or Epic Poem

d. An instructional/technical document

e. A religious text

37. What point of view is this passage told in?

a. First person

b. Second person

c. Third person objective

d. Third person limited

e. Third person omniscient

Questions 38–50 are based on the following passage:

In the quest to understand existence, modern philosophers must question if humans can fully comprehend the world. Classical western approaches to philosophy tend to hold that one can understand something, be it an event or object, by standing outside of the phenomena and observing it. It is then by unbiased observation that one can grasp the details of the world. This seems to hold true for many things. Scientists conduct experiments and record their findings, and thus many natural phenomena become comprehendible. However, several of these observations were possible because humans used tools in order to make these discoveries.

This may seem like an extraneous matter. After all, people invented things like microscopes and telescopes in order to enhance their capacity to view cells or the movement of stars. While humans are still capable of seeing things, the question remains if human beings have the capacity to fully observe and see the world in order to understand it. It would not be an impossible stretch to argue that what humans see through a microscope is not the exact thing itself, but a human interpretation of it.

This would seem to be the case in the "Business of the Holes" experiment conducted by Richard Feynman. To study the way electrons behave, Feynman set up a barrier with two holes and a plate. The plate was there to indicate how many times the electrons would pass through the hole(s). Rather than casually observe the electrons acting under normal circumstances, Feynman discovered that electrons behave in two totally different ways depending on whether or not they are observed. The electrons that were observed had passed through either one of the holes or were caught on the plate as particles. However, electrons that weren't observed acted as waves instead of particles and passed through both holes. This indicated that electrons have a dual nature. Electrons seen by the human eye act like particles, while unseen electrons act like waves of energy.

This dual nature of the electrons presents a conundrum. While humans now have a better understanding of electrons, the fact remains that people cannot entirely perceive how electrons behave without the use of instruments. We can only observe one of the mentioned behaviors, which only provides a partial understanding of the entire function of electrons. Therefore, we're forced to ask ourselves whether the world we observe is objective or if it is subjectively perceived by humans. Or, an alternative question: can man understand the world only through machines that will allow them to observe natural phenomena?

Both questions humble man's capacity to grasp the world. However, those ideas don't consider that many phenomena have been proven by human beings without the use of machines, such as the discovery of gravity. Like all philosophical questions, whether man's reason and observation alone can understand the universe can be approached from many angles.

38. The word *extraneous* in paragraph two can be best interpreted as referring to which one of the following?
   a. Indispensable
   b. Bewildering
   c. Superfluous
   d. Exuberant
   e. Unorthodox

39. What is the author's motivation for writing the passage?
   a. To bring to light an alternative view on human perception by examining the role of technology in human understanding.
   b. To educate the reader on the latest astroparticle physics discovery and offer terms that may be unfamiliar to the reader.
   c. To argue that humans are totally blind to the realities of the world by presenting an experiment that proves that electrons are not what they seem on the surface.
   d. To reflect on opposing views of human understanding.
   e. To present a catalogue of philosophers and what they believe concerning quantum physics.

40. Which of the following most closely resembles the way in which paragraph four is structured?
   a. It offers one solution, questions the solution, and then ends with an alternative solution.
   b. It presents an inquiry, explains the details of that inquiry, and then offers a solution.
   c. It presents a problem, explains the details of that problem, and then ends with more inquiry.
   d. It gives a definition, offers an explanation, and then ends with an inquiry.
   e. It offers an explanation, presents an inquiry, then offers a response to the inquiry.

41. For the classical approach to understanding to hold true, which of the following must be required?
   a. A telescope
   b. A recording device
   c. Multiple witnesses present
   d. A specific understanding of the approach
   e. The person observing must be unbiased

42. Which best describes how the electrons in the experiment behaved like waves?
   a. The electrons moved up and down like actual waves.
   b. The electrons passed through both holes and then onto the plate.
   c. The electrons converted to photons upon touching the plate.
   d. Electrons were seen passing through one hole or the other.
   e. The electrons turned to liquid once they passed through the holes.

43. The author mentions "gravity" in the last paragraph in order to do what?

a. To show that different natural phenomena test man's ability to grasp the world.

b. To prove that since man has not measured it with the use of tools or machines, humans cannot know the true nature of gravity.

c. To demonstrate an example of natural phenomena humans discovered and understand without the use of tools or machines.

d. To show an alternative solution to the nature of electrons that humans have not thought of yet.

e. To show the challenges that gravity presents to studying electrons and other matter.

44. Which situation best parallels the revelation of the dual nature of electrons discovered in Feynman's experiment?

a. A man is born color-blind and grows up observing everything in lighter or darker shades. With the invention of special goggles he puts on, he discovers that there are other colors in addition to different shades.

b. The coelacanth was thought to be extinct, but a live specimen was just recently discovered. There are now two living species of coelacanth known to man, and both are believed to be endangered.

c. In the Middle Ages, blacksmiths added carbon to iron, thus inventing steel. The consequences of this important discovery would have its biggest effects during the industrial revolution.

d. In order to better examine and treat broken bones, the x-ray machine was invented and put to use in hospitals and medical centers.

e. Penicillin was discovered on accident by Alexander Fleming. Fleming noticed that the bacteria in a Petri dish was being stopped by the mold.

45. Which statement about technology would the author likely disagree with?

a. Technology can help expand the field of human vision.

b. Technology renders human observation irrelevant.

c. Developing tools used in observation and research indicates growing understanding of our world itself.

d. Studying certain phenomena necessitates the use of tools and machines.

e. Tools have been used for centuries to observe and understand the world around us.

46. As it is used in paragraph 4, the word *conundrum* most nearly means:

a. platitude

b. enigma

c. solution

d. hypothesis

e. inquiry

47. What is the author's purpose in paragraph 3?

a. To prove to the audience the thesis of the passage by providing evidence suggesting that electrons behave differently when observed by the human eye.

b. To propose that the experiment conducted was not ethically done and to provide evidence that a new experiment should be conducted in order to reach the truth.

c. To introduce the topic to the audience in a manner that puts it into a practical as well as historical understanding.

d. To pose a question relating to the topic about whether humans fully observe phenomena in an objective or subjective sense.

e. To try and answer difficult questions and propose that there are still many different ways to approach these questions.

48. What type of writing would this be considered?
    a. Descriptive
    b. Persuasive
    c. Informational
    d. Instructional
    e. Narrative

49. What type of text would you find this passage in?
    a. Dictionary
    b. Mythology
    c. Science fiction
    d. Fictional novel
    e. Scientific essay

50. What type of rhetorical device is used in paragraph 4?
    a. Metaphor
    b. Simile
    c. Hyperbole
    d. Rhetorical question
    e. Onomatopoeia

Answer Explanations

1. B: Strong dislike. This vocabulary question can be answered using context clues and common sense. Based on the rest of the conversation, the reader can gather that Albert isn't looking forward to his marriage. As the Count notes that "you don't appear to me to be very enthusiastic on the subject of this marriage," and also remarks on Albert's "objection to a young lady who is both rich and beautiful," readers can guess Albert's feelings. The answer choice that most closely matches "objection" and "not . . . very enthusiastic" is *B*, "strong dislike."

2. C: Their name is more respected than the Danglars'. This inference question can be answered by eliminating incorrect answers. Choice *A* is tempting, considering that Albert mentions money as a concern in his marriage. However, although he may not be as rich as his fiancée, his father still has a stable income of 50,000 francs a year. Choice *B* isn't mentioned at all in the passage, so it's impossible to make an inference. Choices *D* and *E* are both false because Albert's father arranged his marriage but his mother doesn't approve of it. Evidence for Choice *C* can be found in the Count's comparison of Albert and Eugénie: "she will enrich you, and you will ennoble her." In other words, the Danglars are wealthier, but the Morcerf family has a more noble background.

3. D: Apprehensive. As in question 7, there are many clues in the passage that indicate Albert's attitude towards his marriage—far from enthusiastic, he has many reservations. This question requires test takers to understand the vocabulary in the answer choices. "Pragmatic" is closest in meaning to "realistic," and "indifferent" means "uninterested." The word "animosity" is a bit strong, meaning extreme anger. The only word related to feeling worried, uncertain, or unfavorable about the future is "apprehensive."

4. B: He is like a wise uncle, giving practical advice to Albert. Choice *A* is incorrect because the Count's tone is friendly and conversational. Choice *C* is also incorrect because the Count questions why Albert doesn't want to marry a young, beautiful, and rich girl. While the Count asks many questions, he isn't particularly "probing" or "suspicious"—instead, he's asking to find out more about Albert's situation and then give him advice about marriage. The two men are not strangers, as the count does offer Albert some advice on his marriage.

5. A: She belongs to a noble family. Though Albert's mother doesn't appear in the scene, there's more than enough information to answer this question. More than once is his family's noble background mentioned (not to mention that Albert's mother is the Comtesse de Morcerf, a noble title). The other answer choices can be eliminated—she is obviously deeply concerned about her son's future; money isn't her highest priority because otherwise she would favor a marriage with the wealthy Danglars; she is not supportive of her son's marriage; and Albert describes her "clear and penetrating judgment," meaning she makes good decisions.

6. E: The richest people in society were also the most respected. The Danglars family is wealthier but the Morcerf family has a more aristocratic name, which gives them a higher social standing. Evidence for the other answer choices can be found throughout the passage: Albert mentioned receiving money from his father's fortune after his marriage; Albert's father has arranged this marriage for him; and the Count speculates that Albert's mother disapproves of this marriage because Eugénie isn't from a noble background like the Morcerf family, implying that she would prefer a match with a girl from aristocratic society.

7. A: He seems reluctant to marry Eugénie, despite her wealth and beauty. This is a reading comprehension question, and the answer can be found in the following lines: '"I confess," observed Monte Cristo, "that I have some difficulty in comprehending your objection to a young lady who is both rich and beautiful."' Choice *B* is the opposite (Albert's father is the one who insists on the marriage), Choice *C* incorrectly represents Albert's eagerness to marry, Choice *D* describes a more positive attitude than Albert actually feels ("repugnance"), and Choice *E* is not talked about in this passage.

8. B: The passage is mostly made up of dialogue. We can see this in the way the two characters communicate with each other, in this case through the use of quotations marks, or dialogue. Narration is when the narrator (not the characters) is explaining things that are happening in the story. Description is when the narrator describes a specific setting and its images. Explanation is when the author is analyzing or defining something for the reader's benefit. Informational text is when the author is simply presenting information to an audience.

9. D: The meaning of the word "ennoble" in the middle of the paragraph means to give someone a noble rank or title. In the passage, we can infer that Albert is noble but not rich, and Mademoiselle Eugénie is rich but not noble.

10. C: Because he finally understands Albert's point of view but still doesn't agree with it. The other choices aren't mentioned anywhere in the passage. Remember, although this passage is part of a larger text, the test taker should only pay attention to what's in the passage itself in order to find the correct answer.

11. E: Albert's father, the Comte de Morcerf, is a soldier. This information is provided in the middle longest paragraph, starting with the line, "'That, perhaps, might not be considered a large sum, in Paris especially,' said the count."

12. E: This text most likely belongs to a fiction novel. For this question we can do a process of elimination. Choices *A* and *D* are incorrect; an autobiography or biography has an informative or expository style, rather than a whole page of dialogue. Choice *B*, drama, is incorrect, because a drama usually gives stage direction or has the speaker of the text out in front of the dialogue rather than in quotes. Choice *C* is incorrect because epic poems are narrower on the page and are usually in some sort of iambic pentameter or metrical lines. This text most likely belongs to a fiction novel due to the nature of the dialogue.

13. C: In lines 6 and 7, it is stated that avarice can prevent a man from being necessitously poor, but too timorous, or fearful, to achieve real wealth. According to the passage, avarice does tend to make a person very wealthy. The passage states that oppression, not avarice, is the consequence of wealth. The passage does not state that avarice drives a person's desire to be poor. Choice *E* is not mentioned in the text.

14. D: Paine believes that the distinction that is beyond a natural or religious reason is between king and subjects. He states that the distinction between good and bad is made in heaven. The distinction between male and female is natural. He does not mention anything about the distinction between humans and animals or faith and fear.

15. A: The passage states that the Heathens were the first to introduce government by kings into the world. The quiet lives of patriarchs came before the Heathens introduced this type of government. It was Christians, not Heathens, who paid divine honors to living kings. Heathens honored deceased kings.

Equal rights of nature and the Mosaic account of creation are mentioned in the paragraph, but not in relation to the Heathens.

16. B: Paine asserts that a monarchy is against the equal rights of nature and cites several parts of scripture that also denounce it. He doesn't say it is against the laws of nature. Because he uses scripture to further his argument, it is not despite scripture that he denounces the monarchy. Paine addresses the law by saying the courts also do not support a monarchical government.

17. A: To be *idolatrous* is to worship idols or heroes, in this case, kings. It is not defined as being deceitful. While idolatry is considered a sin, it is an example of a sin, not a synonym for it. Idolatry may have been considered illegal in some cultures, but it is not a definition for the term.

18. A: The essential meaning of the passage is that the Almighty, God, would disapprove of this type of government. While heaven is mentioned, it is done so to suggest that the monarchical government is irreverent, not that heaven isn't promised. God's disapproval is mentioned, not his punishment. The passage refers to the Jewish monarchy, which required both belief in God and kings.

19. A: The word *timorous* means being full of fear. The author concludes that extreme greed (avarice) makes people too afraid to be prosperous.

20. B: The author's attitude is closest to Choice *B*, impassioned and critical. Choice *A* is incorrect; the author is not indifferent or fatigued—on the contrary, there is a lot of energy and some underlying passion in the writing. Choice *C* is incorrect; the word *enchanted* means delighted, and the author is more critical and concerned of a monarchial government than enchanted with it. Choice *D* is not the best answer; although the author is passionate and critical of a monarchy, there is more logic than anger coming from the words. Choice *E* is incorrect; the author would not be writing a persuasive essay if he were *contented*, which means satisfied.

21. B: To explain how monarchs came into existence and how Christians adapted to this way of government. Choice *A* is incorrect; the author does not agree that heathens were more advanced than Christians in this paragraph, it only explains the catalyst of the monarchial systems. Choice *C* is incorrect; the author would in fact disagree with the divination of the English monarchs. Choice *D* is incorrect; the paragraph *does* believe that monarchs cause damage, but the paragraph does not act as a counterargument to the one preceding it. Choice *E* is incorrect; this is a description of the third paragraph, not the fourth.

22. D: The author implies that the recorded history of creation is a collection, collage, or pattern taken from various accounts of cultures. Choice *A* is incorrect; there is no talk of cells or biology in the paragraph. Since "mosaic" modifies the word "account," we know that it is the account of creation that is mosaic, not creation itself, which makes Choice *B* incorrect. Choice *C* is also incorrect; the paragraph does not mention kings developing a system of recording accounts of creation. Choice *E* is incorrect, as there is no reason the author means to describe creation as comforting.

23. E: This text is most likely an essay, Choice *E*. An essay is usually an informative text about a specific kind of subject. In this case, the text is a political essay about the danger of monarchs. Choice *A*, a diary, would be much more personal and written in the first person. Choice *B*, biography, would be about a specific person's life and achievements. Choice *C*, autobiography, would be the author talking about himself and his own life in an objective tone. Choice *D*, speech, usually addresses an audience at the beginning, and this text does not.

24. D: The purpose of this pamphlet is to convince those who are in the American colonies to become aware of the pitfalls of British monarchy so that more support could be added to gain independence from that monarchy. Therefore, the audience would be individuals who are on the fence about the best way to govern a country.

25. B: The first paragraph explains the difficulties facing the group of travelers. Language and making a living are listed in the second sentence, so Choices *A* and *C* are both incorrect. Extra fees and exorbitant rates are described in the first paragraph's final sentence; therefore, Choice *D* is incorrect. Although the men were later separated from their wives and children, that separation was due to a problem with logistics. There was no prohibition specifically against bringing their wives and children. The entire group was legally barred from leaving the country. Choice *E* is incorrect; we can see how the travelers were treated during their travels, especially in the second paragraph. Thus, Choice *B* is the correct answer.

26. B: The Dutchman's swears his "sacramente" near the end of the third paragraph, and the preceding phrase describes it as "his countries oath." Although "sacramente" sounds like a religious prayer or ritual, it's specifically described as an oath; therefore, Choices *A, C,* and *E* are incorrect. The Dutchman promises to take the group to the commune, but that's not what the "sacramente" is specifically referencing; therefore, Choice *D* is also incorrect. Thus, Choice *B* is the correct answer.

27. D: The ship hired at Boston in Lincoln-shire is the group's first attempt to flee their homeland, and it's described in the second paragraph. After the group reached an agreement with the shipmaster, he betrayed them to the government, which led to government officials arresting the group. The women didn't become sick or get separated until their second attempt at fleeing, so Choices *A* and *B* are both incorrect. Following the first shipmaster's betrayal, the group did go to jail, but their imprisonment occurred after their first attempt to leave went wrong; therefore, Choice *C* is incorrect. There is no shipwreck in this passage, so Choice *E* is incorrect. Thus, Choice *D* is the correct answer.

28. A: After the men boarded the ship, armed government officials arrived on the shore. Rather than risk everyone getting caught, the Dutch shipmaster raised the anchor, hoisted the sails, and took off. So, even though the men were moved to tears by the separation, there was nothing they could do. The government refused to let some of the group's member out of prison, but that's not what caused the separation; therefore, Choice *B* is incorrect. Choices *C, D,* and *E* are factually incorrect based on the information contained in the third paragraph. Thus, Choice *A* is the correct answer.

29. C: Ships charged the group of travelers extra fees because the government outlawed their departure. The first paragraph says that the government barred them from the ports and havens, so they needed to find a secret passage out of the country. As helping the group was illegal, ships charged them extra fees in exchange for taking on that risk. The passage doesn't state why the group is being persecuted; therefore, Choice *A* is incorrect. Choice *B* is incorrect because the passage doesn't mention whether the voyage was particularly long or dangerous. While the government does seize property from the group, it's unclear whether the group is particularly wealthy; therefore, Choice *D* is incorrect. Choice *E* is incorrect because nothing is mentioned about the group being rowdy. Thus, Choice *C* is the correct answer.

30. D: The government repeatedly tried to stop the group from leaving. Government officials prohibited the group from entering the ports, arrested the group after their first shipmaster's betrayal, imprisoned the group for attempting to leave, and sent armed soldiers to thwart their second attempt. The government did the opposite of expelling the group; therefore, Choice *A* is incorrect. It's unclear why the government is persecuting the group, so Choices *B* and *E* are incorrect. Although the government does ultimately capture the women and children, it's because they're the only people left on the shore, not because the government values them more; therefore, Choice *C* is incorrect. Thus, Choice *D* is the correct answer.

31. E: Following the first shipmaster's betrayal, the group was arrested, and the government officials paraded them through the street to embarrass them. The group's imprisonment occurred after the embarrassing parade; therefore, Choice *A* is incorrect. A shipwreck never occurred, so Choice *B* is incorrect. The men cried and the women became sick during the group's second attempt at fleeing their homeland. This occurs after the embarrassing parade through town and subsequent imprisonment; therefore, Choices *C* and *D* are both incorrect. Thus, Choice *E* is the correct answer.

32. A: The second paragraph begins with the group reaching an agreement with a shipmaster at Boston in Lincoln-shire. The rest of the paragraph describes the shipmaster's betrayal, government officials parading the group through the town in an embarrassing way, and the group being imprisoned. The group did receive better treatment from the magistrates than the lords of the counsel while in prison, but Choice *B* only describes the end of the paragraph, so it is incorrect. The women don't get sick until the third paragraph; therefore, Choice *C* is incorrect. Choice *D* is incorrect because it only summarizes the second paragraph's last sentence. Choice *E* is not found anywhere in the passage. Thus, Choice *A* is the correct answer.

33. D: At the end of the passage, the men were brought to tears after armed government officials arrested their wives and children. Given that the group had already been imprisoned for attempting to flee their homeland, it's reasonable to infer that their wives and children would receive the same or worse treatment. As such, there was a strong likelihood that the men wouldn't see their wives and children for a long time.

34. B: The wives and children became separated from the men after the women got sick on the way to the meeting place. As a result, the women's boat took a detour, and they weren't ready in time to board the ship before armed government officials arrived on the shore. While some of the group's members were still in prison, many of the wives and children intended to make the voyage; therefore, Choice *A* is incorrect. The captain of the second ship never betrayed them, so Choice *C* is incorrect. The group took a detour due to the women getting sick, not because of strong winds, so Choice *D* is incorrect. Choice *E* is incorrect because the plan was to arrive with the families together and intact. Thus, Choice *B* is the correct answer.

35. C: The text is from the 1600s and displays how the English language has changed over time. Middle English was from 1150 to 1500, so by the time this account was written, the language was slowly changing into Early Modern English, which lasted from the 1540s to about 1650.

36. A: We can see that this text records parts of history, so this is most likely a historical memoir or the author's personal journal retelling an event that happened. We see the date it was written into (1608) as well as a brief summary of the event before the passage begins.

37. C: This account is told in third person objective voice. First person uses "I" or "we," which is not shown in the passage, so Choice *A* is incorrect. Second person uses "you," which is not represented in the passage, so Choice *B* is incorrect. Choice *D* is third person but only within the confines of *one* character, and we see many characters being represented here. Choice *E* means that we have unlimited views into the minds of all characters, not just their actions, so this is incorrect.

38. C: *Extraneous* most nearly means *superfluous*, or *trivial*. Choice *A*, *indispensable*, is incorrect because it means the opposite of *extraneous*. Choice *B*, *bewildering*, means *confusing* and is not relevant to the context of the sentence. Choice *D* is wrong because although the prefix of the word is the same, *ex-*, the word *exuberant* means *elated* or *enthusiastic*, and is irrelevant to the context of the sentence. Choice *E* is incorrect because *unorthodox* means not conforming to rules.

39. A: The author's purpose is to bring to light an alternative view on human perception by examining the role of technology in human understanding. This is a challenging question because the author's purpose is somewhat open-ended. The author concludes by stating that the questions regarding human perception and observation can be approached from many angles. Thus, the author does not seem to be attempting to prove one thing or another. Choice *B* is incorrect because we cannot know for certain whether the electron experiment is the latest discovery in astroparticle physics because no date is given. Choice *C* is a broad generalization that does not reflect accurately on the writer's views. While the author does appear to reflect on opposing views of human understanding (Choice *D*), the best answer is Choice *A*. Choice *E* is incorrect; although philosophers are mentioned in the first paragraph, they are meant to supplement an introductory concept rather than be the subject of the whole essay.

40. C: It presents a problem, explains the details of that problem, and then ends with more inquiry. The beginning of this paragraph literally "presents a conundrum," explains the problem of partial understanding, and then ends with more questions, or inquiry. There is no solution offered in this paragraph, making Choices *A and B* incorrect. Choice *D* is incorrect because the paragraph does not begin with a definition. The paragraph also has the inquiry at the end with no response after, making Choice *E* incorrect.

41. E: Looking back in the text, the author describes that classical philosophy holds that understanding can be reached by careful observation. This will not work if they are overly invested or biased in their pursuit. Choices *A*, *B*, and *C* are in no way related and not mentioned in the text. A specific theory is not necessary to understanding, according to classical philosophy mentioned by the author, making Choice *D* incorrect.

42. B: The electrons passed through both holes and then onto the plate. Choices *A* and *C* are incorrect because such movement is not mentioned at all in the text. In the passage the author says that electrons that were physically observed appeared to pass through one hole or another. Remember, the electrons that were observed doing this were described as acting like particles. Therefore, Choice *D* is incorrect. The text does not mention electrons turning to liquid, making Choice *E* incorrect. Recall that the plate actually recorded electrons passing through both holes simultaneously and hitting the plate. This behavior, the electron activity that wasn't seen by humans, was characteristic of waves. Thus, Choice *B* is the right answer.

43. C: The author mentions "gravity" to demonstrate an example of natural phenomena humans discovered and understand without the use of tools or machines. Choice *A* mirrors the language in the beginning of the paragraph but is incorrect in its intent. Choice *B* is incorrect; the paragraph mentions nothing of "not knowing the true nature of gravity." Choices *D* and *E* are incorrect as well. There is no mention of an "alternative solution" in this paragraph, and gravitational challenges pertaining to electrons are not mentioned.

44. A: The important thing to keep in mind is that we must choose a scenario that best parallels, or is most similar to, the discovery of the experiment mentioned in the passage. The important aspects of the experiment can be summed up like so: humans directly observed one behavior of electrons and then through analyzing a tool (the plate that recorded electron hits), discovered that there was another electron behavior that could not be physically seen by human eyes. This summary best parallels the scenario in Choice *A*. Like Feynman, the colorblind person can observe one aspect of the world, but through the special goggles (a tool), he is able to see a natural phenomenon that he could not physically see on his own.

45. B: The author would not agree that technology renders human observation irrelevant. Choice *A* is incorrect because much of the passage discusses how technology helps humans observe what cannot be seen with the naked eye; therefore, the author would agree with this statement. This line of reasoning is also why the author would agree with Choice *D*, making it incorrect as well. As indicated in the second paragraph, the author seems to think that humans create inventions and tools with the goal of studying phenomena more precisely. This indicates increased understanding as people recognize limitations and develop items to help bypass the limitations and learn. Therefore, Choice *C* is incorrect as well. Again, the author doesn't attempt to disprove or dismiss classical philosophy. Choice *E* is incorrect; the author talks about telescopes and microscopes that have been around for centuries.

46. B: The word *conundrum* most nearly means *enigma*, which is a mystery or riddle. *Platitude* means a banal or overused saying. *Solution* is incorrect here; and *hypothesis* implies a theory or assumption, so this is also incorrect. *Inquiry* implied that a question has been asked.

47. A: To prove to the audience the thesis of the passage by providing evidence suggesting that electrons behave differently when observed by the human eye. The thesis' best evidence is found in this paragraph because of the experiment depicting how electrons behave in a dual nature. Choice *B* is incorrect; the paragraph mentions nothing about the experiment being unethical. Choice *C* is incorrect; this is characteristic of the first paragraph. Choice *D* is incorrect; this is more characteristic of the second paragraph. Choice *E* is incorrect; this is more characteristic of the last paragraph.

48. C: This would be considered informational writing. Informational writing presents information about a certain subject, and is popular in the science field because it remains unbiased and is concerned with presenting facts to the reader.

49. E: You would find this passage in a scientific essay because it provides an unbiased description of a scientific process meant to inform an audience. A dictionary is used to give definitions to words, making Choice *A* incorrect. Mythology is a collection of stories and folktale that contribute to a culture's literature, usually including creation myths or explaining phenomena. Science fiction is usually fictional accounts of futuristic or alternative worlds, making Choice *C* incorrect. Choice *D* is based on storytelling, so this is incorrect.

50. D: Paragraph 4 presents a rhetorical question at the very end. Rhetorical question are useful for engaging with the audience and encouraging them to think about the information in a new way. Metaphor is saying something is equivalent to another thing, so Choice *A* is incorrect. Simile is saying that something is *like* another thing, so Choice *B* is incorrect. Hyperbole is an extreme exaggeration of something, so Choice *C* is incorrect. Onomatopoeia is when a literal sound sounds like the word itself, like BOOM or CRUNCH, so this is incorrect.

Free-Response

Writing a Response

Brainstorming

One of the most important steps in writing an essay is prewriting. Before drafting an essay, it's helpful to think about the topic for a moment or two, in order to gain a more solid understanding of what the task is. Then, spending about five minutes jotting down the immediate ideas that could work for the essay is recommended. It is a way to get some words on the page and offer a reference for ideas when drafting. Scratch paper is provided for writers to use any prewriting techniques such as webbing, free writing, or listing. The goal is to get ideas out of the mind and onto the page.

Considering Opposing Viewpoints

In the planning stage, it's important to consider all aspects of the topic, including different viewpoints on the subject. There are more than two ways to look at a topic, and a strong argument considers those opposing viewpoints. Considering opposing viewpoints can help writers present a fair, balanced, and informed essay that shows consideration for all readers. This approach can also strengthen an argument by recognizing and potentially refuting the opposing viewpoint(s).

Drawing from personal experience may help to support ideas. For example, if the goal for writing is a personal narrative, then the story should be from the writer's own life. Many writers find it helpful to draw from personal experience, even in an essay that is not strictly narrative. Personal anecdotes or short stories can help to illustrate a point in other types of essays as well.

Moving from Brainstorming to Planning

Once the ideas are on the page, it's time to turn them into a solid plan for the essay. The best ideas from the brainstorming results can then be developed into a more formal outline. An outline typically has one main point (the thesis) and at least three sub-points that support the main point. Here's an example:

<u>Main Idea</u>

- Point #1
- Point #2
- Point #3

Of course, there will be details under each point, but this approach is the best for dealing with timed writing.

Staying on Track

Basing the essay on the outline aids in both organization and coherence. The goal is to ensure that there is enough time to develop each sub-point in the essay, roughly spending an equal amount of time on each idea. Keeping an eye on the time will help. If there are fifteen minutes left to draft the essay, then it makes sense to spend about 5 minutes on each of the ideas. Staying on task is critical to success, and timing out the parts of the essay can help writers avoid feeling overwhelmed.

Parts of the Essay

The *introduction* has to do a few important things:

- Establish the *topic* of the essay in original wording (i.e., not just repeating the prompt)
- Clarify the significance/importance of the topic or purpose for writing (not too many details, a brief overview)
- Offer a *thesis statement* that identifies the writer's own viewpoint on the topic (typically one-two brief sentences as a clear, concise explanation of the main point on the topic)

Body paragraphs reflect the ideas developed in the outline. Three-four points is probably sufficient for a short essay, and they should include the following:

- A *topic sentence* that identifies the sub-point (e.g., a reason why, a way how, a cause or effect)
- A detailed *explanation* of the point, explaining why the writer thinks this point is valid
- Illustrative examples, such as personal examples or real-world examples, that support and validate the point (i.e., "prove" the point)
- A *concluding sentence* that connects the examples, reasoning, and analysis to the point being made

The *conclusion*, or final paragraph, should be brief and should reiterate the focus, clarifying why the discussion is significant or important. It is important to avoid adding specific details or new ideas to this paragraph. The purpose of the conclusion is to sum up what has been said to bring the discussion to a close.

Precision

People often think of precision in terms of math, but precise word choice is another key to successful writing. Since language itself is imprecise, it's important for the writer to find the exact word or words to convey the full, intended meaning of a given situation. For example:

> The number of deaths has gone down since seat belt laws started.

There are several problems with this sentence. First, the word *deaths* is too general. From the context, it's assumed that the writer is referring only to deaths caused by car accidents. However, without clarification, the sentence lacks impact and is probably untrue. The phrase *gone down* might be accurate, but a more precise word would provide more information and greater accuracy. Did the numbers show a slow and steady decrease in highway fatalities or a sudden drop? If the latter is true, the writer is missing a chance to make his or her point more dramatically. Instead of *gone down* the author could substitute *plummeted, fallen drastically*, or *rapidly diminished* to bring the information to life. Also, the phrase *seat belt laws* is unclear. Does it refer to laws requiring cars to include seat belts or to laws requiring drivers and passengers to use them? Finally, *started* is not a strong verb. Words like *enacted* or *adopted* are more direct and make the content more real. When put together, these changes create a far more powerful sentence:

> The number of highway fatalities has plummeted since laws requiring seat belt usage were enacted.

However, it's important to note that precise word choice can sometimes be taken too far. If the writer of the sentence above takes precision to an extreme, it might result in the following:

> The incidence of high-speed, automobile accident-related fatalities has decreased 75% and continued to remain at historical lows since the initial set of federal legislations requiring seat belt use were enacted in 1992.

This sentence is extremely precise, but it takes so long to achieve that precision that it suffers from a lack of clarity. Precise writing is about finding the right balance between information and flow. This is also an issue of conciseness (discussed in the next section).

The last thing for writers to consider with precision is a word choice that's not only unclear or uninteresting, but also confusing or misleading. For example:

> The number of highway fatalities has become hugely lower since laws requiring seat belt use were enacted.

In this case, the reader might be confused by the word *hugely*. Huge means large, but here the writer uses *hugely* in an incorrect and awkward manner. Although most readers can decipher this, doing so disconnects them from the flow of the writing and makes the writer's point less effective.

Concision

"Less is more" is a good rule for writers to follow when composing a sentence. Unfortunately, writers often include extra words and phrases that seem necessary at the time but add nothing to the main idea. This confuses the reader and creates unnecessary repetition. Writing that lacks conciseness is usually guilty of excessive wordiness and redundant phrases. Here's an example containing both of these issues:

> When legislators decided to begin creating legislation making it mandatory for automobile drivers and passengers to make use of seat belts while in cars, a large number of them made those laws for reasons that were political reasons.

There are several empty or "fluff" words here that take up too much space. These can be eliminated while still maintaining the writer's meaning. For example:

- *decided to begin* could be shortened to *began*
- making it mandatory for could be shortened to requiring
- *make use of* could be shortened to *use*
- *a large number* could be shortened to *many*

In addition, there are several examples of redundancy that can be eliminated:

- legislators decided to begin creating legislation and made those laws
- automobile drivers and passengers and while in cars
- reasons that were political reasons

These changes are incorporated as follows:

> When legislators began requiring drivers and passengers to use seat belts, many of them did so for political reasons.

There are many general examples of redundant phrases, such as *add an additional, complete and total, time schedule*, and *transportation vehicle*. If asked to identify a redundant phrase on the exam, test takers should look for words that are close together with the same (or similar) meanings.

Don't Panic!

Writing an essay can be overwhelming, and performance panic is a natural response. The outline serves as a basis for the writing and helps to keep writers focused. Getting stuck can also happen, and it's helpful to remember that brainstorming can be done at any time during the writing process. Following the steps of the writing process is the best defense against writer's block.

Timed essays can be particularly stressful, but assessors are trained to recognize the necessary planning and thinking for these timed efforts. Using the plan above and sticking to it helps with time management. Timing each part of the process helps writers stay on track. Sometimes writers try to cover too much in their essays. If time seems to be running out, this is an opportunity to determine whether all of the ideas in the outline are necessary. Three body paragraphs are sufficient, and more than that is probably too much to cover in a short essay.

More isn't always *better* in writing. A strong essay will be clear and concise. It will avoid unnecessary or repetitive details. It is better to have a concise, five-paragraph essay that makes a clear point, than a ten-paragraph essay that doesn't. The goal is to write one-two pages of quality writing. Paragraphs should also reflect balance; if the introduction goes to the bottom of the first page, the writing may be going off-track or be repetitive. It's best to fall into the one-two page range, but a complete, well-developed essay is the ultimate goal.

The Final Steps

Leaving a few minutes at the end to revise and proofread offers an opportunity for writers to polish things up. Putting one's self in the reader's shoes and focusing on what the essay actually says helps writers identify problems—it's a movement from the mindset of writer to the mindset of editor. The goal is to have a clean, clear copy of the essay. The following areas should be considered when proofreading:

- Sentence fragments
- Awkward sentence structure
- Run-on sentences
- Incorrect word choice
- Grammatical agreement errors
- Spelling errors
- Punctuation errors
- Capitalization errors

The Short Overview

The essay may seem challenging, but following these steps can help writers focus:

- Take one-two minutes to think about the topic.
- Generate some ideas through brainstorming (three-four minutes).
- Organize ideas into a brief outline, selecting just three-four main points to cover in the essay (eventually the body paragraphs).
- Develop essay in parts.
- Introduction paragraph, with intro to topic and main points.
- Viewpoint on the subject at the end of the introduction.
- Body paragraphs, based on outline.
- Each paragraph: makes a main point, explains the viewpoint, uses examples to support the point.
- Brief conclusion highlighting the main points and closing.
- Read over the essay (last five minutes).
- Look for any obvious errors, making sure that the writing makes sense.

Conventions of Standard English

Syntax

Syntax refers to the arrangement of words, phrases, and clauses to form a sentence. Knowledge of syntax can also give insight into a word's meaning. Here is an example of how the placement of a word can impact its meaning and grammatical function:

A. The development team has reserved the conference room for today.

B. Her quiet and reserved nature is sometimes misinterpreted as unfriendliness when people first meet her.

In addition to using *reserved* to mean different things, each sentence also uses the word to serve a different grammatical function. In sentence A, *reserved* is part of the verb phrase *has reserved,* indicating the meaning "to set aside for a particular use." In sentence B, *reserved* acts as a modifier within the noun phrase "her quiet and reserved nature." Because the word is being used as an adjective to describe a personality characteristic, it calls up a different definition of the word—"restrained or lacking familiarity with others." As this example shows, the function of a word within the overall sentence structure can allude to its meaning. It is also useful to refer to a chart about suffixes and parts of speech as another clue into what grammatical function a word is serving in a sentence.

Sentence Structure and Formation

Sentence Structure

Simple sentence: composed of one independent clause

Many people watch hummingbirds.

Note that it has one subject and one verb; however, a simple sentence can have a compound subject and/or a compound verb.

Adults and children often enjoy watching and photographing hummingbirds.

Compound sentence: composed of two independent clauses

The wind knocked down lots of trees, but no trees in my yard were affected.

Complex sentence: composed of one independent clause and one dependent clause

Although the wind knocked down lots of trees, no trees in my yard were affected.

Sentence Fluency

Learning and utilizing the mechanics of structure will encourage effective, professional results, and adding some creativity will elevate one's writing to a higher level.

First, the basic elements of sentences will be reviewed.

A **sentence** is a set of words that make up a grammatical unit. The words must have certain elements and be spoken or written in a specific order to constitute a complete sentence that makes sense.

1. A sentence must have a **subject** (a noun or noun phrase). The subject tells whom or what the sentence is addressing (i.e. what it is about).

2. A sentence must have an **action** or **state of being** (*a* verb). To reiterate: A verb forms the main part of the predicate of a sentence. This means that it explains what the noun is doing.

3. A sentence must convey a complete thought.

When examining writing, readers should be mindful of grammar, structure, spelling, and patterns. Sentences can come in varying sizes and shapes, so the point of grammatical correctness is not to stamp out creativity or diversity in writing. Rather, grammatical correctness ensures that writing will be enjoyable and clear. One of the most common methods successful test takers employ to catch errors is to mouth the words as they read them. Many typos are fixed automatically by the brain, but mouthing the words often circumvents this instinct and helps one read what's actually on the page. Often, grammar errors are caught not by memorization of grammar rules but by the training of one's mind to know whether something *sounds* right or not.

Types of Sentences

There isn't an overabundance of absolutes in grammar, but here is one: every sentence in the English language falls into one of four categories.

Declarative: a simple statement that ends with a period

The price of milk per gallon is the same as the price of gasoline.

Imperative: a command, instruction, or request that ends with a period

Buy milk when you stop to fill up your car with gas.

Interrogative: a question that ends with a question mark

Will you buy the milk?

Exclamatory: a statement or command that expresses emotions like anger, urgency, or surprise and ends with an exclamation mark

Buy the milk now!

Declarative sentences are the most common type, probably because they are comprised of the most general content, without any of the bells and whistles that the other three types contain. They are, simply, declarations or statements of any degree of seriousness, importance, or information.

Imperative sentences often seem to be missing a subject. The subject is there, though; it is just not visible or audible because it is *implied*. For example:

Buy the milk when you fill up your car with gas.

In this sentence, *you* is the implied subject, the one to whom the command is issued. This is sometimes called *the understood you* because it is understood that *you* is the subject of the sentence.

Interrogative sentences—those that ask questions—are defined as such from the idea of the word **interrogation**, the action of questions being asked of suspects by investigators. Although that is serious business, interrogative sentences apply to all kinds of questions.

To exclaim is at the root of **exclamatory** sentences. These are made with strong emotions behind them. The only technical difference between a declarative or imperative sentence and an exclamatory one is the exclamation mark at the end. The example declarative and imperative sentences can both become an exclamatory one simply by putting an exclamation mark at the end of the sentences.

The price of milk per gallon is the same as the price of gasoline!

Buy milk when you stop to fill up your car with gas!

After all, someone might be really excited by the price of gas or milk, or they could be mad at the person that will be buying the milk! However, as stated before, exclamation marks in abundance defeat their own purpose! After a while, they begin to cause fatigue! When used only for their intended purpose, they can have their expected and desired effect.

Transitions

Transitions are the glue used to make organized thoughts adhere to one another. Transitions are the glue that helps put ideas together seamlessly, within sentences and paragraphs, between them, and (in longer documents) even between sections. Transitions may be single words, sentences, or whole paragraphs (as in the prior example). Transitions help readers to digest and understand what to feel about what has gone on and clue readers in on what is going on, what will be, and how they might react to all these factors. Transitions are like good clues left at a crime scene.

Parallel Structure in a Sentence

Parallel structure, also known as **parallelism**, refers to using the same grammatical form within a sentence. This is important in lists and for other components of sentences.

> Incorrect: At the recital, the boys and girls were dancing, singing, and played musical instruments.
>
> Correct: At the recital, the boys and girls were dancing, singing, and playing musical instruments.

Notice that in the first example, *played* is not in the same verb tense as the other verbs nor is it compatible with the helping verb *were*. To test for parallel structure in lists, try reading each item as if it were the only item in the list.

> The boys and girls were dancing.
>
> The boys and girls were singing.
>
> The boys and girls were played musical instruments.

Suddenly, the error in the sentence becomes very clear. Here's another example:

Incorrect: After the accident, I informed the police *that Mrs. Holmes backed* into my car, *that Mrs. Holmes got out* of her car to look at the damage, and *she was driving* off without leaving a note.

Correct: After the accident, I informed the police *that Mrs. Holmes backed* into my car, *that Mrs. Holmes got out* of her car to look at the damage, and *that Mrs. Holmes drove off* without leaving a note.

Correct: After the accident, I informed the police that Mrs. Holmes *backed* into my car, *got out* of her car to look at the damage, and *drove off* without leaving a note.

Note that there are two ways to fix the nonparallel structure of the first sentence. The key to parallelism is consistent structure.

Punctuation

Ellipses

An **ellipsis** (. . .) consists of three handy little dots that can speak volumes on behalf of irrelevant material. Writers use them in place of words, lines, phrases, list content, or paragraphs that might just as easily have been omitted from a passage of writing. This can be done to save space or to focus only on the specifically relevant material.

> Exercise is good for some unexpected reasons. Watkins writes, "Exercise has many benefits such as . . . reducing cancer risk."

In the example above, the ellipsis takes the place of the other benefits of exercise that are more expected.

The ellipsis may also be used to show a pause in sentence flow.

> "I'm wondering . . . how this could happen," Dylan said in a soft voice.

<u>Commas</u>

A **comma** (,) is the punctuation mark that signifies a pause—breath—between parts of a sentence. It denotes a break of flow. As with so many aspects of writing structure, authors will benefit by reading their writing aloud or mouthing the words. This can be particularly helpful if one is uncertain about whether the comma is needed.

In a complex sentence—one that contains a **subordinate (dependent)** clause or clauses—the use of a comma is dictated by where the subordinate clause is located. If the subordinate clause is located before the main clause, a comma is needed between the two clauses.

> I will not pay for the steak, *because I don't have that much money.*

Generally, if the subordinate clause is placed after the main clause, no punctuation is needed.

> I did well on my exam because I studied two hours the night before.

Notice how the last clause is dependent because it requires the earlier independent clauses to make sense.

Use a comma on both sides of an interrupting phrase.

> I will pay for the ice cream, chocolate and vanilla, and then will eat it all myself.

The words forming the phrase in italics are nonessential (extra) information. To determine if a phrase is nonessential, try reading the sentence without the phrase and see if it's still coherent.

A comma is not necessary in this next sentence because no interruption—nonessential or extra information—has occurred. Read sentences aloud when uncertain.

> I will pay for his chocolate and vanilla ice cream and then will eat it all myself.

If the nonessential phrase comes at the beginning of a sentence, a comma should only go at the end of the phrase. If the phrase comes at the end of a sentence, a comma should only go at the beginning of the phrase.

Other types of interruptions include the following:

- interjections: Oh no, I am not going.
- abbreviations: Barry Potter, M.D., specializes in heart disorders.
- direct addresses: Yes, Claudia, I am tired and going to bed.
- parenthetical phrases: His wife, lovely as she was, was not helpful.
- transitional phrases: Also, it is not possible.

The second comma in the following sentence is called an Oxford comma.

> I will pay for ice cream, syrup, and pop.

It is a comma used after the second-to-last item in a series of three or more items. It comes before the word *or* or *and*. Not everyone uses the Oxford comma; it is optional, but many believe it is needed. The comma functions as a tool to reduce confusion in writing. So, if omitting the Oxford comma would cause confusion, then it's best to include it.

Commas are used in math to mark the place of thousands in numerals, breaking them up so they are easier to read. Other uses for commas are in dates (*March 19, 2016*), letter greetings (*Dear Sally,*), and in between cities and states (*Louisville, KY*).

Semicolons

The **semicolon** (;) might be described as a heavy-handed comma. Take a look at these two examples:

> I will pay for the ice cream, but I will not pay for the steak.
> I will pay for the ice cream; I will not pay for the steak.

What's the difference? The first example has a comma and a conjunction separating the two independent clauses. The second example does not have a conjunction, but there are two independent clauses in the sentence, so something more than a comma is required. In this case, a semicolon is used.

Two independent clauses can only be joined in a sentence by either a comma and conjunction or a semicolon. If one of those tools is not used, the sentence will be a run-on. Remember that while the clauses are independent, they need to be closely related in order to be contained in one sentence.

Another use for the semicolon is to separate items in a list when the items themselves require commas.

> The family lived in Phoenix, Arizona; Oklahoma City, Oklahoma; and Raleigh, North Carolina.

Colons

Colons (:) have many miscellaneous functions. Colons can be used to proceed further information or a list. In these cases, a colon should only follow an independent clause.

> Humans take in sensory information through five basic senses: sight, hearing, smell, touch, and taste.

The meal includes the following components:

- Caesar salad
- spaghetti
- garlic bread
- cake

The family got what they needed: a reliable vehicle.

While a comma is more common, a colon can also proceed a formal quotation.

> He said to the crowd: "Let's begin!"

The colon is used after the greeting in a formal letter.

Dear Sir:
To Whom It May Concern:

In the writing of time, the colon separates the minutes from the hour (*4:45 p.m.*). The colon can also be used to indicate a ratio between two numbers (*50:1*).

Hyphens

The **hyphen** (-) is a little hash mark that can be used to join words to show that they are linked.

Hyphenate two words that work together as a single adjective (a compound adjective).

honey-covered biscuits

Some words always require hyphens, even if not serving as an adjective.

merry-go-round

Hyphens always go after certain prefixes like *anti-* & *all-*.

Hyphens should also be used when the absence of the hyphen would cause a strange vowel combination (*semi-engineer*) or confusion. For example, *re-collect* should be used to describe something being gathered twice rather than being written as *recollect*, which means to remember.

Parentheses and Dashes

Parentheses are half-round brackets that look like this: *( )*. They set off a word, phrase, or sentence that is an afterthought, explanation, or side note relevant to the surrounding text but not essential. A pair of commas is often used to set off this sort of information, but parentheses are generally used for information that would not fit well within a sentence or that the writer deems not important enough to be structurally part of the sentence.

The picture of the heart (see above) shows the major parts you should memorize.

Mount Everest is one of three mountains in the world that are over 28,000 feet high (K2 and Kanchenjunga are the other two).

See how the sentences above are complete without the parenthetical statements? In the first example, *see above* would not have fit well within the flow of the sentence. The second parenthetical statement could have been a separate sentence, but the writer deemed the information not pertinent to the topic.

The **dash** (—) is a mark longer than a hyphen used as a punctuation mark in sentences and to set apart a relevant thought. Even after plucking out the line separated by the dash marks, the sentence will be intact and make sense.

Looking out the airplane window at the landmarks—Lake Clarke, Thompson Community College, and the bridge—she couldn't help but feel excited to be home.

The dashes use is similar to that of parentheses or a pair of commas. So, what's the difference? Many believe that using dashes makes the clause within them stand out while using parentheses is subtler. It's advised to not use dashes when commas could be used instead.

Quotation Marks

Here are some instances where **quotation marks** should be used:

- Dialogue for characters in narratives. When characters speak, the first word should always be capitalized and the punctuation goes inside the quotes. For example:

    Janie said, "The tree fell on my car during the hurricane."

- Around titles of songs, short stories, essays, and chapter in books.
- To emphasize a certain word.
- To refer to a word as the word itself.

Apostrophes

This punctuation mark, the apostrophe ('), is a versatile little mark. It has a few different functions:

- Quotes: Apostrophes are used when a second quote is needed within a quote.
    - In my letter to my friend, I wrote, "The girl had to get a new purse, and guess what Mary did? She said, 'I'd like to go with you to the store.' I knew Mary would buy it for her."
- Contractions: Another use for an apostrophe in the quote above is a contraction. *I'd* is used for *I would.*
- Possession: An apostrophe followed by the letter *s* shows possession (*Mary's* purse). If the possessive word is plural, the apostrophe generally just follows the word.
    - The trees' leaves are all over the ground.

Usage

Spelling might or might not be important to some, or maybe it just doesn't come naturally, but those who are willing to discover some new ideas and consider their benefits can learn to spell better and improve their writing. Misspellings reduce a writer's credibility and can create misunderstandings. Spell checkers built into word processors are not a substitute for accuracy. They are neither foolproof nor without error. In addition, a writer's misspelling of one word may also be a valid (but incorrect) word. For example, a writer intending to spell *herd* might accidentally type *s* instead of *d* and unintentionally spell *hers*. Since *her*s is a word, it would not be marked as a misspelling by a spell checker. In short, writers should use spell check, but not rely on them.

Guidelines for Spelling

Saying and listening to a word serves as the beginning of knowing how to spell it. Writers should keep these subsequent guidelines in mind, remembering there are often exceptions because the English language is replete with them.

Guideline #1: Syllables must have at least one vowel. In fact, every syllable in every English word has a vowel.

- d*o*g
- h*a*yst*a*ck
- *a*nsw*e*r*i*ng
- *a*bst*e*nt*iou*s
- s*i*mpl*e*

Guideline #2: The long and short of it. When the vowel has a short vowel sound as in *mad* or *bed,* only the single vowel is needed. If the word has a long vowel sound, add another vowel, either alongside it or separated by a consonant: bed/*bead*; mad/*made.* When the second vowel is separated by two spaces—*madder*—it does not affect the first vowel's sound.

Guideline #3: Suffixes. Refer to the examples listed above.

Guideline #4: Which comes first; the *i* or the *e*? Remember the saying, "*I* before *e* except after *c* or when sounding as *a* as in *neighbor* or *weigh*." Keep in mind that these are only guidelines and that there are always exceptions to every rule.

Guideline #5: Vowels in the right order. Another helpful rhyme is, "When two vowels go walking, the first one does the talking." When two vowels are in a row, the first one often has a long vowel sound and the other is silent. An example is *team*.

If one has difficulty spelling words, he or she can determine a strategy to help. Some people work on spelling by playing word games like Scrabble or Words with Friends. Others use phonics, which is sounding words out by slowly and surely stating each syllable. People try repeating and memorizing spellings as well as picturing words in their head, or they may try making up silly memory aids. Each person should experiment and see what works best.

Homophones

Homophones are two or more words that have no particular relationship to one another except their identical pronunciations. Homophones make spelling English words fun and challenging. Examples include:

Common Homophones	
affect, effect	eminent, imminent
allot, a lot	flew, flu, flue
barbecue, barbeque	gauge, gage
bite, byte	holy, wholly
brake, break	it's, its
capital, capitol	knew, new
cash, cache	libel, liable
cell, sell	principal, principle
colonel, kernel	their, there, they're
do, due, dew	to, too, two
dual, duel	yoke, yolk

Irregular Plurals

Irregular plurals are words that aren't made plural the usual way.

- Most nouns are made plural by adding *–s* (book*s*, television*s*, skyscraper*s*).
- Most nouns ending in *ch, sh, s, x,* or *z* are made plural by adding *–es* (church*es*, marsh*es*).
- Most nouns ending in a vowel + *y* are made plural by adding *–s* (day*s*, toy*s*).
- Most nouns ending in a consonant + *y,* are made plural by the *-y* becoming *-ies* (baby becomes *babies*).

- Most nouns ending in an *o* are made plural by adding *–s* (pian*os,* phot*os*).
- Some nouns ending in an *o*, though, may be made plural by adding *–es* (example: potato*es,* volcano*es*), and, of note, there is no known rhyme or reason for this!
- Most nouns ending in an *f* or *fe* are made plural by the *-f* or *-fe* becoming *-ves*! (example: wolf becomes *wolves*).
- Some words function as both the singular and plural form of the word (fish, deer).
- Other exceptions include *man* becomes *men, mouse* becomes *mice, goose* becomes *geese,* and *foot* becomes *feet.*
- Contractions

The basic rule for making **contractions** is one area of spelling that is pretty straightforward: combine the two words by inserting an apostrophe (') in the space where a letter is omitted. For example, to combine *you* and *are*, drop the *a* and put the apostrophe in its place: *you're.*

he + is = he's

you + all = y'all (informal, but often misspelled)

Note that *it's*, when spelled with an apostrophe, is always the contraction for *it is*. The possessive form of the word is written without an apostrophe as *its*.

Rhetorical Analysis

Aristotelian Rhetorical Analysis

Also known as the **Five Rhetorical Canons**, Aristotelian rhetorical analysis takes into consideration the various methods used to effectively persuade an audience using an oral platform. Aristotle, the great philosopher and rhetorician, lived in a time where most persuasion was done out loud in front of an audience. He used these canons as a guideline to effective speech and how to eloquently draw in an audience. Let's look at the five canons below:

- **Invention**: Invention can be seen as the first step in creating effective rhetoric. The speaker's relationship with the audience is important to this step, as the speaker uses this connection to invent the best possible way to reach his or her audience. Additionally, speakers should contemplate what the best possible medium is for their particular audience. Does the audience want a story? Would they be better receptive to a more ironical work, like a satire? Or would they want something serious and straightforward, like a description or analysis? Invention is how the speaker shapes his or her message in relation to an audience.

- **Arrangement**: The arrangement of a text is how the speaker chooses to organize the information presented. What should come first, and how should the rest of the text logically follow? Thinking about the audience is extremely important to arrangement, especially their position on the issue. A speaker would not want to approach a hostile audience by stating the opposite viewpoint straight away; the speaker would subtly and thoughtfully lead the audience to come to their own conclusion on an issue after all of the facts and rhetorical appeals are presented.

- **Style**: The style of a text is where the speaker's creative expression comes in. Or, as in technical or instructional writing, creative expression might be stifled for clarity's sake. The style of writing is the speaker/writer's lack or presence of creative expression and personality. Different ways to use style in speaking include tone, diction, figurative language, and word choice.

- **Memory**: Memory in rhetoric refers to the speaker being able to *recall* certain forms of memory or knowledge about their topic in case the audience has questions or asks the speaker to explain more on the subject. Memory is about the speaker's credibility and prior knowledge. Memory can also be about the speaker's knowledge of the audience and what *their* memory might entail, such as their own prior knowledge and assumptions they might have about the issue.

- **Delivery**: Delivery speaks to the credibility of the speaker or writer through *how* they deliver their message. Do they use proper syntax and punctuation? What is their timing like? Do they open with a proper introduction and end with a memorable conclusion? Does the delivery in the speech or writing involve excitement and passion, or is it critical and dull? Delivery is important to a speaker/author's credibility because good delivery relies on assessment of placement and timing.

Making Generalizations Based on Evidence

One way to make generalizations is to look for main topics. When doing so, pay particular attention to any titles, headlines, or opening statements made by the author. Topic sentences or repetitive ideas can be clues in gleaning inferred ideas. For example, if a passage contains the phrase *DNA testing, while some consider it infallible, is an inherently flawed technique,* the test taker can infer the rest of the passage will contain information that points to DNA testing's infallibility.

The test taker may be asked to make a generalization based on prior knowledge but may also be asked to make predictions based on new ideas. For example, the test taker may have no prior knowledge of DNA other than its genetic property to replicate. However, if the reader is given passages on the flaws of DNA testing with enough factual evidence, the test taker may arrive at the inferred conclusion or generalization that the author does not support the infallibility of DNA testing in all identification cases.

When making generalizations, it is important to remember that the critical thinking process involved must be fluid and open to change. While a reader may infer an idea from a main topic, general statement, or other clues, they must be open to receiving new information within a particular passage. New ideas presented by an author may require the test taker to alter a generalization. Similarly, when asked questions that require making an inference, it's important to read the entire test passage and all of the answer options. Often, a test taker will need to refine a generalization based on new ideas that may be presented within the text itself.

Textual evidence within the details helps readers draw a conclusion about a passage. **Textual evidence** refers to information—facts and examples that support the main point. Textual evidence will likely come from outside sources and can be in the form of quoted or paraphrased material. In order to draw a conclusion from evidence, it's important to examine the credibility and validity of that evidence as well as how (and if) it relates to the main idea.

If an author presents a differing opinion or a **counterargument** in order to refute it, the reader should consider how and why this information is being presented. It is meant to strengthen the original argument and shouldn't be confused with the author's intended conclusion, but it should also be considered in the reader's final evaluation.

Text Credibility

Credible sources are important when drawing conclusions because readers need to be able to trust what they are reading. Authors should always use credible sources to help gain the trust of their readers. A text is *credible* when it is believable and the author is objective and unbiased. If readers do not trust an author's words, they may simply dismiss the text completely. For example, if an author writes a persuasive essay, he or she is outwardly trying to sway readers' opinions to align with his or her own. Readers may agree or disagree with the author, which may, in turn, lead them to believe that the author is credible or not credible. Also, readers should keep in mind the source of the text. If readers review a journal about astronomy, would a more reliable source be a NASA employee or a medical doctor? Overall, text credibility is important when drawing conclusions, because readers want reliable sources that support the decisions they have made about the author's ideas.

Examining Paragraphs

While authors write, thoughts coalesce to form words on "paper" (aka a computer screen). Authors strategically place those thoughts in sentences to give them "voice" in an orderly manner, and then they manipulate them into cohesive sentences for cohesion to express ideas. Like a hunk of modeling clay (thanks to computers, people are no longer bound to erasers and whiteout), sentences can be worked and reworked until they cooperate and say what was originally intended.

Before calling a paragraph complete, identify its main point, making sure that related sentences stay on point. Pose questions such as, "Did I sufficiently develop the main point? Did I say it succinctly enough? Did I give it time to develop? *Is* it developed?"

Let's examine the following two paragraphs, each an example of a movie review. Read them and form a critique.

> Example 1: *Eddie the Eagle* is a movie about a struggling athlete. Eddie was crippled at birth. He had a lot of therapy and he had a dream. Eddie trained himself for the Olympics. He went far away to learn how to ski jump. It was hard for him, but he persevered. He got a coach and kept trying. He qualified for the Olympics. He was the only one from Britain who could jump. When he succeeded, they named him, "Eddie the Eagle."

> Example 2: The last movie I saw in the theater was *Eddie the Eagle,* a story of extraordinary perseverance inspired by real life events. Eddie was born in England with a birth defect that he slowly but surely overcame, but not without trial and error (not the least of which was his father's perpetual *dis*couragement). In fact, the old man did everything to get him to give up, but Eddie was dogged beyond anyone in the neighborhood; in fact, maybe beyond anyone in the whole town or even the whole world! Eddie, simply, did not know to quit. As he grew up, so did his dream; a strange one, indeed, for someone so unaccomplished: to compete in the Winter Olympics as a ski jumper (which he knew absolutely nothing about). Eddie didn't just keep on dreaming about it. He actually went to Germany and *worked* at it, facing unbelievable odds, defeats, and put-downs by Dad and the other Men in Charge, aka the Olympic decision-makers. Did that stop him? No way! Eddie got a coach and persevered. Then, when he failed, he persevered some more, again and again. You should be able to open up a dictionary, look at the

word "persevere," and see a picture of Eddie the Eagle because, when everybody told him he couldn't, he did. The result? He is forever dubbed, "Eddie the Eagle."

Both reviews tell something about the movie *Eddie the Eagle*. Does one motivate the reader to want to see the movie more than the other? Does one just provide a few facts while the other paints a virtual picture of the movie? Does one give a carrot and the other a rib eye steak, mashed potatoes, and chocolate silk pie?

Paragraphs sometimes only give facts. Sometimes that's appropriate and all that is needed. Sometimes, though, writers want to use the blank documents on their computer screens to paint a picture. Writers must "see" the painting come to life. To do so, pick a familiar topic, write a simple sentence, and add to it. Pretend, for instance, there's a lovely view. What does one see? Is it a lake? Try again – picture it as though it were the sea! Visualize a big ship sailing out there. Is it sailing away or approaching? Who is on it? Is it dangerous? Is it night and are there crazy pirates on board? Uh-oh! Did one just jump ship and start swimming toward shore?

Synthesis

Authentic Inquiry

Synthesis in reading involves the ability to fully comprehend text passages, and then going further by making new connections to see things in a new or different way. It involves a full thought process and requires readers to change the way they think about what they read. The Accuplacer will require a test taker to integrate new information that he or she already knows and demonstrate an ability to express new thoughts.

Synthesis goes further than summary. When summarizing, a reader collects all of the information an author presents in a text passage and restates it in an effective manner. Synthesis requires that the test taker not only summarize reading material but be able to express new ideas based on the author's message. It is a full culmination of all reading comprehension strategies. It will require the test taker to order, recount, summarize, and recreate information into a whole new idea.

In utilizing synthesis, a reader must be able to form mental images about what they read, recall any background information they have about the topic, ask critical questions about the material, determine the importance of points an author makes, make inferences based on the reading, and finally be able to form new ideas based on all of the above skills. Synthesis requires the reader to make connections, visualize concepts, determine their importance, ask questions, make inferences, then fully synthesize all of this information into new thought.

Linking the Sources

When analyzing two or more texts, there are several different aspects that need to be considered, particularly the styles (or the artful way in which the authors use diction to deliver a theme), points of view, and types of argument. In order to do so, one should compare and contrast the following elements between the texts:

- Style: narrative, persuasive, descriptive, informative, etc.
- Tone: sarcastic, angry, somber, humorous, etc.
- Sentence structure: simple (1 clause) compound (2 clauses), complex-compound (3 clauses)
- Punctuation choice: question marks, exclamation points, periods, dashes, etc.

- Point of view: first person, second person, third person
- Paragraph structure: long, short, both, differences between the two
- Organizational structure: compare/contrast, problem/solution, chronological, etc.

The following two passages concern the theme of death and are presented to demonstrate how to evaluate the above elements:

Passage I

Death occurs in several stages. The first stage is the pre-active stage, which occurs a few days to weeks before death, in which the desire to eat and drink decreases, and the person may feel restless, irritable, and anxious. The second stage is the active stage, where the skin begins to cool, breathing becomes difficult as the lungs become congested (known as the "death rattle"), and the person loses control of their bodily fluids.

Once death occurs, there are also two stages. The first is clinical death, when the heart stops pumping blood and breathing ceases. This stage lasts approximately 4-6 minutes, and during this time, it is possible for a victim to be resuscitated via CPR or a defibrillator. After 6 minutes however, the oxygen stores within the brain begin to deplete, and the victim enters biological death. This is the point of no return, as the cells of the brain and vital organs begin to die, a process that is irreversible.

Passage II

It was her sister Josephine who told her, in broken sentences; veiled hints that revealed in half concealing. Her husband's friend Richards was there, too, near her. It was he who had been in the newspaper office when intelligence of the railroad disaster was received, with Brently Mallard's name leading the list of "killed." He had only taken the time to assure himself of its truth by a second telegram, and had hastened to forestall any less careful, less tender friend in bearing the sad message.

She did not hear the story as many women have heard the same, with a paralyzed inability to accept its significance. She wept at once, with sudden, wild abandonment, in her sister's arms. When the storm of grief had spent itself, she went away to her room alone. She would have no one follow her.

There stood, facing the open window, a comfortable, roomy armchair. Into this she sank, pressed down by a physical exhaustion that haunted her body and seemed to reach into her soul.

Excerpt from "The Story of an Hour" by Kate Chopin

Now, using the outline above, the similarities and differences between the two passages are considered:

1. **Style:** Passage I is an expository style, presenting purely factual evidence on death, completely devoid of emotion. Passage II is a narrative style, where the theme of death is presented to us by the reaction of the loved ones involved. This narrative style is full of emotional language and imagery.

2. **Tone:** Passage I has no emotionally-charged words of any kind, and seems to view death simply as a process that happens, neither welcoming nor fearing it. The tone in this passage, therefore, is neutral. Passage II does not have a neutral tone—it uses words like "disaster," "killed," "sad," "wept," "wild abandonment," and "physical exhaustion," implying an anxiety toward the theme of death.

3. **Sentence Structure:** Passage I contains many complex-compound sentences, which are used to accommodate lots of information. The structure of these sentences contributes to the overall informative nature of the selection. Passage II has several compound sentences and complex sentences on their own. It's also marked by the use of many commas in a single sentence, separating modifying words. Perhaps this variety is meant to match the sporadic emotion of the character's discovery of her husband's death.

4. **Punctuation Choice:** Passage I uses only commas and periods, which adds to the overall neutral tone of the selection. Passage II mostly uses commas and periods, and then one semicolon. Again, the excess of commas and semicolon in the first sentence may be said to mirror the character's anxiety.

5. **Point of View:** Passage I uses third-person point of view, as it avoids any first- or second-person pronouns. Passage II also uses third-person point of view, as the story is being told by a narrator about characters separate from the narrator.

6. **Paragraph Structure:** The first passage is told in an objective way, and each paragraph is focused on the topic brought up in the first sentence. The second passage has no specific topic per paragraph. It is organized in a sequential way, so the paragraphs flow into the next in a chronological order.

7. **Organizational Structure:** The structure of Passage I is told in a very objective, organized way. The first paragraph tells of the stages before death, and the second paragraph tells of the stages after death. The second passage is told in chronological order, as a sequence of events, like in a fictional story.

When analyzing the different structures, it may be helpful to make a table and use single words to compare and contrast the texts:

Elements	**Passage I**	**Passage II**
Style	Expository	Narrative
Tone	Neutral	Emotional
Sentence Structure	Long	Long/Sporadic
Punctuation Choice	.	. and ,
Point of View	Third	Third
Paragraph Structure	Focused	Sequential
Organizational Structure	Objective/Logical	Chronological

The main differences between the two selections are style, tone, and structure. Possibly the most noticeable difference is the style and tone, as one tone is more neutral, and the other tone is more emotional. This is due to the word choice used and how each passage treats the topic of death. These are only a handful of the endless possible interpretations the reader could make.

The Source-Informed Argument

<u>Constructing Arguments Through Evidence</u>
Using only one form of supporting evidence is not nearly as effective as using a variety to support a claim. Presenting only a list of statistics can be boring to the reader but providing a true story that's both interesting and humanizing helps. In addition, one example isn't always enough to prove the writer's larger point, so combining it with other examples in the writing is extremely effective. Thus, when reading a passage, readers should not just look for a single form of supporting evidence.

For example, although most people can't argue with the statement, "Seat belts save lives", its impact on the reader is much greater when supported by additional content. The writer can support this idea by:

- Providing statistics on the rate of highway fatalities alongside statistics of estimated seat belt usage.
- Explaining the science behind car accidents and what happens to a passenger who doesn't use a seat belt.
- Offering anecdotal evidence or true stories from reliable sources on how seat belts prevent fatal injuries in car crashes.

Another key aspect of supporting evidence is a **reliable source**. Does the writer include the source of the information? If so, is the source well-known and trustworthy? Is there a potential for bias? For example, a seat belt study done by a seat belt manufacturer may have its own agenda to promote.

Logical Sequence

Even if the writer includes plenty of information to support his or her point, the writing is only effective when the information is in a logical order. **Logical sequencing** is really just common sense, but it's an important writing technique. First, the writer should introduce the main idea, whether for a paragraph, a section, or the entire text. Then he or she should present evidence to support the main idea by using transitional language. This shows the reader how the information relates to the main idea and to the sentences around it. The writer should then take time to interpret the information, making sure necessary connections are obvious to the reader. Finally, the writer can summarize the information in the closing section.

NOTE: Although most writing follows this pattern, it isn't a set rule. Sometimes writers change the order for effect. For example, the writer can begin with a surprising piece of supporting information to grab the reader's attention, and then transition to the main idea. Thus, if a passage doesn't follow the logical order, readers should not immediately assume it's wrong. However, most writing that has a nontraditional beginning usually settles into a logical sequence.

Argumentation

The Steps of an Argument

Strong arguments tend to follow a fairly defined format. In the introduction, background information regarding the problem is shared, the implications of the issue are stated, and the author's thesis or claims are given. Supporting evidence is then presented in the body paragraphs, along with the counterargument, which then gets refuted with specific evidence. Lastly, in the conclusion, the author summarizes the points and claims again.

Evidence Used to Support a Claim or Conclusion

Premises are the why, and **conclusions** are the what. Stated differently, premises are the evidence or facts supporting why the conclusion is logical and valid. ACT Reading questions do not require evaluation of the factual accuracy of the arguments; instead, the questions evaluate the test taker's ability to assess an argument's logical strength. For example, John eats all red food. Apples are red. Therefore, John eats apples. This argument is logically sound, despite having no factual basis in reality. Below is an example of a practice argument.

> Julie is an American track athlete. She's the star of the number one collegiate team in the country. Her times are consistently at the top of national rankings. Julie is extremely likely to represent the United States at the upcoming Olympics.

In this example, the conclusion, or the *what*, is that she will likely be on the American Olympic team. The author supports this conclusion with two premises. First, Julie is the star of an elite track team. Second, she runs some of the best times of the country. This is the *why* behind the conclusion. The following builds off this basic argument:

> Julie is an American track athlete. She's the star of the number one collegiate team in the country. Her times are consistently at the top of national rankings. Julie is extremely likely to represent the United States at the upcoming Olympics. Julie will continue to develop after the Olympic trials. She will be a frontrunner for the gold. Julie is likely to become a world-famous track star.

These additions to the argument make the conclusion different. Now, the conclusion is that Julie is likely to become a world-famous track star. The previous conclusion, Julie will likely be on the Olympic team, functions as a **sub-conclusion** in this argument. Like conclusions, premises must adequately support sub-conclusions. However, sub-conclusions function like premises, since sub-conclusions also support the overall conclusion.

Determining Whether Evidence is Relevant and Sufficient

A **hasty generalization** involves an argument relying on insufficient statistical data or inaccurately generalizing. One common generalization occurs when a group of individuals under observation have some quality or attribute that is asserted to be universal or true for a much larger number of people than actually documented. Here's an example of a hasty generalization:

> A man smokes a lot of cigarettes, but so did his grandfather. The grandfather smoked nearly two packs per day since his World War II service until he died at ninety years of age. Continuing to smoke cigarettes will clearly not impact the grandson's long-term health.

This argument is a hasty generalization because it assumes that one person's addiction and lack of consequences will naturally be reflected in a different individual. There is no reasonable justification for such extrapolation. It is common knowledge that any smoking is detrimental to everyone's health. The fact that the man's grandfather smoked two packs per day and lived a long life has no logical connection with the grandson engaging in similar behavior. The hasty generalization doesn't take into account other reasons behind the grandfather's longevity. Nor does the author offer evidence that might support the idea that the man would share a similar lifetime if he smokes. It might be different if the author stated that the man's family shares some genetic trait rendering them immune to the effects of tar and chemicals on the lungs. If this were in the argument, we would assume it as truth, like everything else in the Reading Through Language Arts section, and find the generalization to be valid rather than hasty. Of course, this is not the case in our example.

Determining Whether a Statement Is or Is Not Supported

The basic tenet of reading comprehension is the ability to read and understand text. One way to understand text is to look for information that supports the author's main idea, topic, or position statement. This information may be factual or it may be based on the author's opinion. This section will focus on the test taker's ability to identify factual information, as opposed to opinionated bias. The ACT will ask test takers to read passages containing factual information, and then logically relate those passages by drawing conclusions based on evidence.

In order to identify factual information within one or more text passages, begin by looking for statements of fact. Factual statements can be either true or false. Identifying factual statements as opposed to opinion statements is important in demonstrating full command of evidence in reading. For example, the statement *The temperature outside was unbearably hot* may seem like a fact; however, it's not. While anyone can point to a temperature gauge as factual evidence, the statement itself reflects only an opinion. Some people may find the temperature unbearably hot. Others may find it comfortably warm. Thus, the sentence, *The temperature outside was unbearably hot,* reflects the opinion of the author who found it unbearable. If the text passage followed up the sentence with atmospheric conditions indicating heat indices above 140 degrees Fahrenheit, then the reader knows there is factual information that supports the author's assertion of *unbearably hot*.

In looking for information that can be proven or disproven, it's helpful to scan for dates, numbers, timelines, equations, statistics, and other similar data within any given text passage. These types of indicators will point to proven particulars. For example, the statement, *The temperature outside was unbearably hot on that summer day, July 10, 1913,* most likely indicates factual information, even if the reader is unaware that this is the hottest day on record in the United States. Be careful when reading biased words from an author. Biased words indicate opinion, as opposed to fact. See the list of biased words below and keep in mind that it's not an inclusive list:

- Great/greatest
- Better/best/worst
- Amazing
- Terrible/bad/awful
- Beautiful/handsome/ugly
- More/most
- Exciting/dull/boring
- Favorite
- Very
- Probably/should/seem/possibly

Remember, most of what is written is actually opinion or carefully worded information that seems like fact when it isn't. To say, *duplicating DNA results is not cost-effective* sounds like it could be a scientific fact, but it isn't. Factual information can be verified through independent sources.

The simplest type of test question may provide a text passage, then ask the test taker to distinguish the correct factual supporting statement that best answers the corresponding question on the test. However, be aware that most questions may ask the test taker to read more than one text passage and identify which answer best supports an author's topic. While the ability to identify factual information is critical, these types of questions require the test taker to identify chunks of details, and then relate them to one another.

Assessing Whether an Argument is Valid

Although different from conditions and If/Then Statements, **reasonableness** is another important foundational concept. Evaluating an argument for reasonableness and validity entails evaluating the evidence presented by the author to justify their conclusions. Everything contained in the argument should be considered, but remember to ignore outside biases, judgments, and knowledge. For the purposes of this test, the test taker is a one-person jury at a criminal trial using a standard of reasonableness under the circumstances presented by the argument.

These arguments are encountered on a daily basis through social media, entertainment, and cable news. An example is:

> Although many believe it to be a natural occurrence, some believe that the red tide that occurs in Florida each year may actually be a result of human sewage and agricultural runoff. However, it is arguable that both natural and human factors contribute to this annual phenomenon. On one hand, the red tide has been occurring every year since the time of explorers like Cabeza de Vaca in the 1500's. On the other hand, the red tide seems to be getting worse each year, and scientists from the Florida Fish & Wildlife Conservation say the bacteria found inside the tide feed off of nutrients found in fertilizer runoff.

The author's conclusion is that both natural phenomena and human activity contribute to the red tide that happens annually in Florida. The author backs this information up by historical data to prove the natural occurrence of the red tide, and then again with scientific data to back up the human contribution to the red tide. Both of these statements are examples of the premises in the argument. Evaluating the strength of the logical connection between the premises and conclusion is how reasonableness is determined. Another example is:

> The local railroad is a disaster. Tickets are exorbitantly priced, bathrooms leak, and the floor is sticky.

The author is clearly unhappy with the railroad service. They cite three examples of why they believe the railroad to be a disaster. An argument more familiar to everyday life is:

> Alexandra said the movie she just saw was amazing. We should go see it tonight.

Although not immediately apparent, this is an argument. The author is making the argument that they should go see the movie. This conclusion is based on the premise that Alexandra said the movie was amazing. There's an inferred note that Alexandra is knowledgeable on the subject, and she's credible enough to prompt her friends to go see the movie. This seems like a reasonable argument. A less reasonable argument is:

> Alexandra is a film student, and she's written the perfect romantic comedy script. We should put our life savings toward its production as an investment in our future.

The author's conclusion is that they should invest their life savings into the production of a movie, and it is justified by referencing Alexandra's credibility and current work. However, the premises are entirely too weak to support the conclusion. Alexandra is only a film *student*, and the script is seemingly her first work. This is not enough evidence to justify investing one's life savings in the film's success.

Assumptions in an Argument

Think of assumptions as unwritten premises. Although they never explicitly appear in the argument, the author is relying on it to defend the argument, just like a premise. Assumptions are the most important part of an argument that will never appear in an argument.

An argument in the abstract is: The author concludes Z based on W and X premises. But the W and X premises actually depend on the unmentioned assumption of Y. Therefore, what the author is really saying is that, X, W, and Y make Z correct, but Y is assumed.

People assume all of the time. Assumptions and inferences allow the human mind to process the constant flow of information. Many assumptions underlie even the most basic arguments. However, in the world of Legal Reasoning arguments, assumptions must be avoided. An argument must be fully presented to be valid; relying on an assumption is considered weak. The test requires that test takers identify these underlying assumptions. One example is:

> Peyton Manning is the most over-rated quarterback of all time. He lost more big games than anyone else. Plus, he allegedly assaulted his female trainer in college. Peyton clearly shouldn't make the Hall of Fame.

The author certainly relies on a lot of assumptions. A few assumptions are:

- Peyton Manning plays quarterback.
- He is considered to be a great quarterback by at least some people.
- He played in many big games.
- Allegations and past settlements without any admission of guilt from over a decade ago can be relied upon as evidence against Hall of Fame acceptance.
- The Hall of Fame voters factor in off-the-field incidents, even if true.
- The best players should make the Hall of Fame.
- Losing big games negates, at least in part, the achievement of making it to those big games
- Peyton Manning is retired, and people will vote on whether he makes the Hall of Fame at some point in the future.

The author is relying on all of these assumptions. Some are clearly more important to his argument than others. In fact, disproving a necessary assumption can destroy a premise and possibly an entire conclusion. For example, what if the Hall of Fame did not factor in any of the off-the-field incidents? Then the alleged assault no longer factors into the argument. Even worse, what if making the big games actually was more important than losing those games in the eyes of the Hall of Fame voters? Then the whole conclusion falls apart and is no longer justified if that premise is disproven.

Assumption questions test this exact point by asking the test taker to identify which assumption the argument relies upon. If the author is making numerous assumptions, then the most important *one* assumption must be chosen.

If the author truly relies on an assumption, then the argument will completely fall apart if the assumption isn't true. **Negating** a necessary assumption will *always* make the argument fall apart. This is a universal rule of logic and should be the first thing done in testing answer choices.

Here are some ways that underlying assumptions will appear as questions:

- Which of the following is a hidden assumption that the author makes to advance his argument?
- Which assumption, if true, would support the argument's conclusion (make it more logical)?
- The strength of the argument depends on which of the following?
- Upon which of the following assumptions does the author rely?
- Which assumption does the argument presuppose?

An example is:

> Frank Underwood is a terrible president. The man is a typical spend, spend, spend liberal. His employment program would exponentially increase the annual deficit and pile on the national debt. Not to mention, Underwood is also on the verge of starting a war with Russia.

Upon which of the following assumptions does the author's argument most rely?

a. Frank Underwood is a terrible president.

b. The United States cannot afford Frank Underwood's policy plans without spending more than the country raises in revenue.

c. No spend, spend, spend liberal has ever succeeded as president.

d. Starting a war with Russia is beneficial to the United States.

Use the negation rule to find the correct answer in the choices below.

Choice *A* is not an assumption—it is the author's conclusion. This type of restatement will never be the correct answer, but test it anyway. After negating the choice, what remains is: *Frank Underwood is a fantastic president*. Does this make the argument fall apart? No, it just becomes the new conclusion. The argument is certainly worse since it does not seem reasonable for someone to praise a president for being a spend, spend, spend liberal or raising the national debt; however, the argument still makes *logical* sense. Eliminate this choice.

Choice *B* is certainly an assumption. It underlies the premises that the country cannot afford Underwood's economic plans. When reversed to: *The United States can afford Frank Underwood's policy plans without spending more than the country raises in revenue,* this destroys the argument. If the United States can afford his plans, then the annual deficit and national debt won't increase; therefore, Underwood being a terrible president would only be based on the final premise. The argument is much weaker without the two sentences involving the financials. Keep it as a benchmark while working through the remaining choices.

Choice *C* is irrelevant. The author is not necessarily claiming that all loose-pocket liberals make for bad presidents. His argument specifically pertains to Underwood. Negate it—*Some spend, spend, spend liberals have succeeded as president.* This does not destroy the argument. Some other candidate could have succeeded as president. However, the author is pointing out that those policies would be disastrous considering the rising budget and debt. The author is not making an appeal to historical precedent. Although not a terrible choice, it is certainly weaker than Choice *B*. Eliminate this choice.

Choice *D* is definitely not an assumption made by the author. The author is assuming that a war with Russia is disastrous. Negate it anyway—*Starting a war with Russia is not beneficial for the United States.* This does not destroy the argument; it makes it stronger. Eliminate this choice.

Analyzing Two Arguments and Evaluating the Types of Evidence Used to Support Each Claim

Arguments use evidence and reasoning to support a position or prove a point. Claims are typically controversial and may be faced with some degree of contention. Thus, authors support claims with evidence. Two arguments might present different types of evidence that readers will need to evaluate for merit, worthiness, accuracy, relevance, and impact. Evidence can take on many forms such as numbers (statistics, measurements, numerical data, etc.), expert opinions or quotes, testimonies, anecdotal evidence or stories from individuals, and textual evidence, such as that obtained from documents like diaries, newspapers, and laws.

Essay Prompts

The free-response section of the AP exam consists of 3 essay prompts. This section makes up 55% of the exam and takes 2 hours and 15 minutes to complete. Responses should be thoughtful and well-organized. Students should spend around 40 minutes on each essay. Test takers should consider writing their thesis statement before crafting any other part of the essay and proofread the essay when done. Essays should be organized with an introduction, several body paragraphs, and then a conclusion. Each prompt is explained below:

Synthesis: The synthesis prompt presents several articles, illustrations, or graphs in regard to one particular topic. It is the test taker's job to read each article and to synthesize the information carefully. After the test taker reads the articles, they should refer to the beginning of the prompt for instructions on crafting an argument.

Rhetorical Analysis: For this prompt, test takers will read a nonfiction text and then analyze how the author's rhetorical choices contribute to the purpose of the text.

Argument: Test takers read about a short topic and then create an evidence-based argument in response to the topic.

Synthesis Prompt

Technology within education has had a dubious role in the past two decades. The use of cell phones and computers is debated regarding whether they may cause a distraction or help aid in learning. However, the conversation in recent years is that technology is hitting our society in full force and can no longer be ignored, especially in education. In fact, studies have found that technology, even the use of video games, may be a positive supplement to learning rather than hindering it. Still, ways in which to use technology are still debated, even the questions of *how much, when* and *what* technology can be used. The articles below provide some discussion and research on the role of technology within education.

Carefully read the following seven sources. Pay attention to the *source* of each image or article, as this tells you where and when the source came from. Then synthesize the information from at least three of the sources and incorporate it into a clear, well-written essay that addresses the question: What is the role of technology within education?

Use the sources to explain and develop your argument. Do not summarize the sources, rather, synthesize them into your own argument. Indicate clearly which sources you are drawing from by using direct quotation, paraphrase, or summary. Cite the sources by saying Source A, Source B, etc., or by using the descriptions in parentheses below.

Source A (Garcia)

Source B (Metz)

Source C (U.S. Dept. of Education 2017)

Source D (Image from Ed Tech)

Source E (Article from Ed Tech)

Source F (U.S. Dept. of Education, 2012)

Source G (Department of eLearning)

Source A

Games for Learning Summit: Expanding the Conversation Between Educators and Game Designers

Whether it is using quick warm-ups like Game of Phones or highly immersive experiences with Mario Kart and Minecraft, digital games can be powerful motivators for learning. It is with this in mind that we are eager to expand the conversation between teachers and game developers.

The U.S. Department of Education and Games for Change, with support from the Entertainment Software Association, will host the Games for Learning Summit April 21 at the 2015 Games for Change (G4C) Festival. With more than 250 participants, including nationally recognized educators, the designers of some of today's most popular video games, and members of the U.S. Department of Education, we are hopeful that this event will encourage collaboration focused on the learning needs and interests of young people in the U.S.

Collaborating and designing with the learning interests of young people in mind requires a shift in thinking from all stakeholders. Based on the conversations we've had with teachers and students, there is a hunger for better games that support better learning today. With the recent release of The Ed Tech Developer's Guide, the pathways for developing for impact are clearer than ever.

At the beginning of the school year, the two of us (along with a handful of amazing teachers) spent a weekend enmeshed with teams of game designers at the White House Education Game Jam. Focused on games that could provide powerful learning resources for schools, we have continued to be optimistic about the results that such collaboration can yield.

A recent game-design project in Chad's classroom highlights some of what game-based learning has to offer us as teachers and students. Inspired by games ranging from Geometry Dash to Sissy's Magical Ponycorn Adventure, students working in teams of four completed their own Scratch games like Wasteland Adventures, World Championship Soccer, and Sanic Pong. Each 'studio' of four students brainstormed genres, tropes, and mechanics for games they wanted to create and play. Then they got to work. Programmers started to code. Artists worked with platforms like Piskel and Google Draw. Sound Engineers scoured freesound.org and Sound Bible for sound effects and composed theme music with Online Sequencer. Student project managers kept everyone working and talking with one another through shared docs and folders.

The project helped students develop media literacy, soft skills like collaboration, and technical skills like managing an online repository of A/V assets, to say nothing of the logic, math, reading, and writing skills they demonstrated in navigating tutorials, communicating online, and building their games. Students even discussed gender norms in character design and traditional gaming narratives. Game-based learning isn't about consuming a product to pick up a fact or two; it's about learning to analyze or produce pieces of interactive media that require critical thinking, persistence, and problem-solving to master, critique, play, and make.

Now, with several White House Education Game Jam alumni and friends coming to the Games for Learning Summit, we are excited about focusing on articulating the thinking, dialogue, and spaces for collaboration between developers and educators.

We're looking forward to continuing conversation far beyond the Games and Learning Summit. We need to work together to answer questions like: How can we help one another make and use games to fulfill educational needs in the classroom? How can we put the best interactive content in the hands of students for the most meaningful educational experiences — those focused on discovery and decision-making? Let's figure out game-changing ways to harness the power of play for the work of learning in schools.

By Antero Garcia, Teaching Ambassador Fellow at the U.S. Department of Education, and Chad Sansing, BETA Academy in Staunton, Virginia "Games for Learning Summit: Expanding the Conversation Between Educators and Game Designers." https://www.data.gov/education/games-for-learning-summit-expanding-the-conversation-between-educators-and-game-designers

Source B

Ed Games Week Highlights the Emergence of Video Games in Education

Games and play are a central part of childhood and can stimulate creativity and learning. As technology grows as a tool for teachers, one question has been: what role might educational video games play in the classroom?

Today, increasing numbers of teachers are incorporating games to supplement and enrich classroom instruction. In addition, students of all ages are developing their own games, as showcased in competitions and hackathons in communities across the country.

Ed Games Week brought the discussion on educational games to Washington, D.C. The Office of Science and Technology Policy (OSTP) and the U.S. Department of Education (ED) collaboratively planned a series of events including the *Ed Games Expo*, the *Ed Games Workshop*, and the *White House Education Game Jam*.

The Ed Games Expo

The Ed Games Expo showcased 25 newly developed learning games developed with funding from the Small Business Innovation Research (SBIR) programs at ED's Institute of Education Sciences (ED/IES SBIR) and other federal programs. More than 150 attendees met face-to-face with the developers and played games that covered a range of topics – from STEM, history, and foreign languages – and used a wide variety of genres for gameplay. For example:

- *Addimal Adventure* challenges children to solve mathematical equations with support of friendly characters.
- *Zoo U* helps grade school students navigate a series of challenging social situations.
- *Reach for the Sun* encourages deep understanding of photosynthesis as students grow a virtual sunflower from seed to full plant.

Ed Games Workshop

The Ed Games Workshop brought together the Expo game developers and a team of federal experts. Workshop collaborators strategized exciting possibilities to create regional, national, or even international STEM game competitions featuring games that motivate as well as teach, such as through an X-Prize model. For more, see this article on the Clinton Foundation blog.

The White House Education Game Jam

Ed Games Week wrapped up with a 48-hour Education Game Jam that brought together over one hundred veteran and independent game developers, teachers, and students with the goal of creating educational games that make challenging K-12 topics easier for students to learn and for teachers to teach. Organized by the White House and Department of Education, developers were challenged to develop playable prototypes during the event. On Monday, Sept. 8, Game Jam participants presented videos of their games and demonstrated the prototypes at the White House. Twenty-three educational games were developed over the weekend including:

- Grub Run, a health and fitness game by Team Pixelopus
- President of the Galaxy, a game about the dynamics of U.S. presidential elections by Team 1st Playable
- Land Grab, a game highlighting a conceptual social behavioral model called the tragedy of the commons, by Team Filamentarians

By Ed Metz, Russell Shilling and Mark DeLoura, "Ed Games Week Highlights the Emergence of Video Games in Education," September 23, 2014, https://www.data.gov/education/ed-games-week-highlights-emergence-video-games-education

Source C

Engaging and Empowering Learning Through Technology

To be successful in our daily lives and in a global workforce, Americans need pathways to acquire expertise and form meaningful connections to peers and mentors. This journey begins with a base of knowledge and abilities that can be augmented and enhanced throughout our lives. Fortunately, advances in learning sciences have provided new insights into how people learn. Technology can be a powerful tool to reimagine learning experiences on the basis of those insights.

Historically, a learner's educational opportunities have been limited by the resources found within the walls of a school. Technology-enabled learning allows learners to tap resources and expertise anywhere in the world, starting with their own communities. For example:

- With high-speed internet access, a student interested in learning computer science can take the course online in a school that lacks the budget or a faculty member with the appropriate skills to teach the course.
- Learners struggling with planning for college and careers can access high-quality online mentoring and advising programs where resources or geography present challenges to obtaining sufficient face-to-face mentoring.
- With mobile data collection tools and online collaboration platforms, students in a remote geographic area studying local phenomena can collaborate with peers doing similar work anywhere in the world.

- A school with connectivity but without robust science facilities can offer its students virtual chemistry, biology, anatomy, and physics labs—offering students learning experiences that approach those of peers with better resources.
- Students engaged in creative writing, music, or media production can publish their work to a broad global audience regardless of where they go to school.
- Technology-enabled learning environments allow less experienced learners to access and participate in specialized communities of practice, graduating to more complex activities and deeper participation as they gain the experience needed to become expert members of the community.

These opportunities expand growth possibilities for all students while affording historically disadvantaged students greater equity of access to high-quality learning materials, expertise, personalized learning, and tools for planning for future education. Such opportunities also can support increased capacity for educators to create blended learning opportunities for their students, rethinking when, where, and how students complete different components of a learning experience.

From the Chapter "Learning: Engaging and Empowering Learning Through Technology," from *Reimagining the Role of Technology in Education* by U.S. Department of Education, January 2017, https://tech.ed.gov/files/2017/01/NETP17.pdf

Source D

TECHNOLOGY CAN FACILITATE SOCIAL INTERACTION

No interaction — Better interaction — Best interaction

From https://tech.ed.gov/earlylearning/principles/

Source E

Guiding Principles for Use of Technology with Early Learners

The Departments recognize that families and early educators have many different options for using technology with early learners. The Departments believe that guidance needs to reflect the reality that families and early educators have access to apps, digital books, games, video chatting software, and a multitude of other interactive technologies that can be used with young children. Even as new technologies emerge, the Departments believe that these principles apply, though guidance may evolve as more research on this topic is published.

The Departments' four guiding principles for use of technology with early learners are as follows:

- Guiding Principle #1: Technology—when used appropriately—can be a tool for learning.
- Guiding Principle #2: Technology should be used to increase access to learning opportunities for all children.
- Guiding Principle #3: Technology may be used to strengthen relationships among parents, families, early educators, and young children.
- Guiding Principle #4: Technology is more effective for learning when adults and peers interact or co-view with young children.

Guiding Principles for Use of Technology with Early Learners, from
https://tech.ed.gov/earlylearning/principles/

Source F

"The Need for Transformation," from *Understanding the Implications of Online Learning for Educational Productivity*

Transforming American Education: Learning Powered by Technology, the most recent U.S. educational technology plan, has set the goal for all levels of the educational system to redesign processes and structures to leverage "the power of technology to improve learning outcomes while making more efficient use of time, money, and staff" (U.S. Department of Education 2010a, 63). The goal suggests that more vigorous efforts are needed to both (1) design and build key constructs and measures that will support increasingly real-time, integrated learning analytics for students, teachers and administrators and (2) develop the technical and human infrastructure needed to plan and implement productivity analyses and use their results appropriately.

To use online learning to its fullest potential, developing online equivalents of existing teaching practices is unlikely to be sufficient (Twigg 1992). Instead, educational decision makers should heed the lessons of other industries and redesign core educational processes. The purpose of the transformation is to sharpen focus on the needs and interests of students as individuals. To the degree possible, instruction should be tailored to meet student goals at their desired pace of learning. Online learning supports diagnostic assessments and frequent and individualized feedback, which may in turn suggest a move toward competency-based systems. In this model, once students demonstrate a desired level of mastery they can move on to new topics and new skills, and savings of time and money can result if they do so at an accelerated pace. Interventions such as these require a fundamental rethinking of the basic parameters of educational systems, but they promise opportunities for significant improvements in productivity.

"The Need for Transformation," from *Understanding the Implications of Online Learning for Educational Productivity*, February 2012 by U.S. Department of Education, https://tech.ed.gov/files/2013/10/implications-online-learning.pdf

Source G

"Technology in the Classroom," From *Digital Literacy*

Every piece of technology, whether it is a mobile phone, a PC, tablet or a pencil needs to have its academic potential considered. Mobile phones are currently a banned device in our schools. It is not just the mobile phone's role that needs to be re-examined but any digital device. For that matter it could also be a textbook, a pencil, a rubber or a ruler. It is important to make a shift to a learning environment in which we challenge our students to communicate their understanding of the curricular objectives or learning outcomes that we are looking for in what ever way that speaks to them. For some students that may be using pen and paper, for some students that may be producing a video while for others it may be creating a presentation. It should be up to the students to determine the best way for them to communicate. Irrespective of the technology in the classroom the real question to be asked is, "Are you on task with that?" Whether you are on task with a pencil or on task with a mobile digital device the question is the same.

From *Digital Literacy: 21st Century Competences for Our Age*, from the chapter "Technology in the Classroom." April 2015. From Department of eLearning, https://education.gov.mt/en/elearning/Documents/Green%20Paper%20Digital%20Literacy%20v6.pdf

Analysis Prompt

The speech below was given by Charles Dickens in Birmingham in England on December 30, 1853 on behalf of the Birmingham and Midland Institute. The speech talks about the working man and the changes the speaker would like to see for the future. Read the speech carefully. Then craft an essay in which you analyze the rhetorical strategies Dickens uses to excite and persuade his audience.

My Good Friends,—When I first imparted to the committee of the projected Institute my particular wish that on one of the evenings of my readings here the main body of my audience should be composed of working men and their families, I was animated by two desires; first, by the wish to have the great pleasure of meeting you face to face at this Christmas time, and accompany you myself through one of my little Christmas books; and second, by the wish to have an opportunity of stating publicly in your presence, and in the presence of the committee, my earnest hope that the Institute will, from the beginning, recognise one great principle—strong in reason and justice—which I believe to be essential to the very life of such an Institution. It is, that the working man shall, from the first unto the last, have a share in the management of an Institution which is designed for his benefit, and which calls itself by his name.

I have no fear here of being misunderstood—of being supposed to mean too much in this. If there ever was a time when any one class could of itself do much for its own good, and for the welfare of society—which I greatly doubt—that time is unquestionably past. It is in the fusion of different classes, without confusion; in the bringing together of employers and employed; in the creating of a better common understanding among those whose interests are identical, who depend upon each other, who are vitally essential to each other, and who never can be in unnatural antagonism without deplorable results, that one of the chief principles of a Mechanics' Institution should consist. In this world a great deal of the bitterness among us arises from an imperfect understanding of one another. Erect in Birmingham a great Educational Institution, properly educational; educational of the feelings as well as of the reason; to which all orders of Birmingham men contribute; in which all orders of Birmingham men meet; wherein all orders of Birmingham men are faithfully represented—and you will erect a Temple of Concord here which will be a model edifice to the whole of England.

Contemplating as I do the existence of the Artisans' Committee, which not long ago considered the establishment of the Institute so sensibly, and supported it so heartily, I earnestly entreat the gentlemen—earnest I know in the good work, and who are now among us,—by all means to avoid the great shortcoming of similar institutions; and in asking the working man for his confidence, to set him the great example and give him theirs in return. You will judge for yourselves if I promise too much for the working man, when I say that he will stand by such an enterprise with the utmost of his patience, his perseverance, sense, and support; that I am sure he will need no charitable aid or condescending patronage; but will readily and cheerfully pay for the advantages which it confers; that he will prepare himself in individual cases where he feels that the adverse circumstances around him have rendered it necessary; in a word, that he will feel his responsibility like an honest man, and will most honestly and manfully discharge it. I now proceed to the pleasant task to which I assure you I have looked forward for a long time.

Argument Prompt

A question that humanity has been asking themselves for a long time is, "Why do we dream?"

Sigmund Freud suggested that dreams are thoughts, desires, and motivations that our unconscious mind expresses while we were asleep. Alternately, Allan Hobson and Robert McCarley in 1977 suggest that dreams are a product of the amygdala and hippocampus being activated while sleeping. These systems effect our memories and emotions, and in turn our brain synthesizes these activations in order to make meaning. The Information-Processing Theory suggests that dreams are a way of processing all the information we have collected from the previous day.

Think about some of the reasons why we might have dreams when we sleep. Then write an essay in which you explain your position on where dreams come from and why we might experience them. Use appropriate evidence from your reading, experience, or observations to support your argument.

Dear AP Comparative Government and Politics Test Taker,

We would like to start by thanking you for purchasing this study guide for your AP Comparative Government and Politics exam. We hope that we exceeded your expectations.

Our goal in creating this study guide was to cover all of the topics that you will see on the test. We also strove to make our practice questions as similar as possible to what you will encounter on test day. With that being said, if you found something that you feel was not up to your standards, please send us an email and let us know.

We would also like to let you know about other books in our catalog that may interest you.

AP Biology

This can be found on Amazon: amazon.com/dp/1628456221

SAT Math 1

amazon.com/dp/1628454717

SAT

amazon.com/dp/1628455217

ACT

amazon.com/dp/162845606X

ACCUPLACER

amazon.com/dp/162845492X

We have study guides in a wide variety of fields. If the one you are looking for isn't listed above, then try searching for it on Amazon or send us an email.

Thanks Again and Happy Testing!
Product Development Team
info@studyguideteam.com

Interested in buying more than 10 copies of our product? Contact us about bulk discounts:

bulkorders@studyguideteam.com

FREE Test Taking Tips DVD Offer

To help us better serve you, we have developed a Test Taking Tips DVD that we would like to give you for FREE. **This DVD covers world-class test taking tips that you can use to be even more successful when you are taking your test.**

All that we ask is that you email us your feedback about your study guide. Please let us know what you thought about it – whether that is good, bad or indifferent.

To get your **FREE Test Taking Tips DVD**, email freedvd@studyguideteam.com with "FREE DVD" in the subject line and the following information in the body of the email:

a. The title of your study guide.

b. Your product rating on a scale of 1-5, with 5 being the highest rating.

c. Your feedback about the study guide. What did you think of it?

d. Your full name and shipping address to send your free DVD.

If you have any questions or concerns, please don't hesitate to contact us at freedvd@studyguideteam.com.

Thanks again!

Made in the
USA
Middletown, DE

76782199R00057